BETH FLINTOFF

Beth Flintoff trained as an actress at Birmingham Conservatoire after studying English Literature at Durham University, and is now a freelance director and playwright. She is an Associate Artist at Reading Between the Lines Theatre Company, for whom she has written *Henry I of England*, *Oscar Wilde on Trial* and *Matilda the Empress*. Her play and theatre installation on Greenham Common, *Greenham: One Hundred Years of War and Peace*, was performed by a cast of hundreds in the middle of the deserted runway in September 2017.

For seven years she worked at The Watermill Theatre, Newbury, where as Outreach Director she worked on many productions as writer, director or both, including *David Copperfield*, *Life Lessons*, *Writers' Block*, *The Girl Who Never Forgot*, *Hamlet*, *Macbeth*, *Romeo and Juliet*, *Othello* and *Doctor Faustus*. She has collaborated twice with physical-theatre ensemble Rhum and Clay, on *Jekyll and Hyde* and *Hardboiled: The Fall of Sam Shadow*, which toured with The Watermill before transferring to New Diorama in London (Off West End Award Nominee for Best Director 2016). Her play *The True History of Susanna Shakespeare* was awarded a Tenancy at Nuffield Southampton Theatres, and longlisted for the Papatango Prize in 2017.

Beth was the founding Artistic Director of new-writing fringe ensemble Debut Theatre Company. She is currently under commission to Reading Between the Lines and Eastern Angles for plays in 2018.

Other Plays for Young People to Perform from Nick Hern Books

Original Plays

100
Christopher Heimann,
   Neil Monaghan, Diene Petterle

BANANA BOYS
Evan Placey

BLOOD AND ICE
Liz Lochhead

BOYS
Ella Hickson

BRAINSTORM
Ned Glasier, Emily Lim
   and Company Three

BUNNY
Jack Thorne

BURYING YOUR BROTHER
   IN THE PAVEMENT
Jack Thorne

COCKROACH
Sam Holcroft

DISCO PIGS
Enda Walsh

EIGHT
Ella Hickson

THE FALL
James Fritz

GIRLS LIKE THAT
Evan Placey

HOLLOWAY JONES
Evan Placey

I CAUGHT CRABS IN WALBERSWICK
Joel Horwood

MOGADISHU
Vivienne Franzmann

MOTH
Declan Greene

THE MYSTAE
Nick Whitby

OVERSPILL
Ali Taylor

PRONOUN
Evan Placey

SAME
Deborah Bruce

THE URBAN GIRL'S GUIDE TO
   CAMPING AND OTHER PLAYS
Fin Kennedy

THE WARDROBE
Sam Holcroft

Adaptations

ANIMAL FARM
Ian Wooldridge
Adapted from George Orwell

ARABIAN NIGHTS
Dominic Cooke

BEAUTY AND THE BEAST
Laurence Boswell

CORAM BOY
Helen Edmundson
Adapted from Jamila Gavin

DAVID COPPERFIELD
Alastair Cording
Adapted from Charles Dickens

GREAT EXPECTATIONS
Nick Ormerod and Declan Donnellan
Adapted from Charles Dickens

HIS DARK MATERIALS
Nicholas Wright
Adapted from Philip Pullman

THE JUNGLE BOOK
Stuart Paterson
Adapted from Rudyard Kipling

KENSUKE'S KINGDOM
Stuart Paterson
Adapted from Michael Morpurgo

KES
Lawrence Till
Adapted from Barry Hines

NOUGHTS & CROSSES
Dominic Cooke
Adapted from Malorie Blackman

THE RAILWAY CHILDREN
Mike Kenny
Adapted from E. Nesbit

SWALLOWS AND AMAZONS
Helen Edmundson and Neil Hannon
Adapted from Arthur Ransome

TO SIR, WITH LOVE
Ayub Khan-Din
Adapted from E.R Braithwaite

TREASURE ISLAND
Stuart Paterson
Adapted from Robert Louis Stevenson

WENDY & PETER PAN
Ella Hickson
Adapted from J.M. Barrie

THE WOLVES OF WILLOUGHBY
   CHASE
Russ Tunney
Adapted from Joan Aiken

Beth Flintoff

THE GLOVE THIEF

NICK HERN BOOKS
www.nickhernbooks.co.uk

TONIC THEATRE
www.tonictheatre.co.uk

A Nick Hern Book

The Glove Thief first published as a paperback original in Great Britain in 2017 by Nick Hern Books Limited, The Glasshouse, 49a Goldhawk Road, London W12 8QP, in association with Tonic

The Glove Thief copyright © 2017 Beth Flintoff

Beth Flintoff has asserted her right to be identified as the author of this work

Cover image by Kathy Barber, Bullet Creative, www.bulletcreative.com
Inside cover image: The Marian Hanging, one of the Oxburgh Hangings at Oxburgh Hall, Norfolk © Victoria and Albert Museum, London

Designed and typeset by Nick Hern Books, London
Printed and bound in Great Britain by Mimeo Ltd, Huntingdon, Cambridgeshire PE29 6XX

A CIP catalogue record for this book is available from the British Library

ISBN   978 1 84842 653 5

Contents

BRIGHT. YOUNG. THINGS. BY GEORGIA CHRISTOU

THE GLOVE THIEF BY BETH FLINTOFF

HEAVY WEATHER BY LIZZIE NUNNERY

THE LIGHT BURNS BLUE BY SILVA SEMERCIYAN

RED BY SOMALIA SEATON

SECOND PERSON NARRATIVE BY JEMMA KENNEDY

THIS CHANGES EVERYTHING BY JOEL HORWOOD

PLATFORM

Commissioning and publishing a range of new plays which give girls a greater share of the action was always on my to-do list when I founded Tonic in 2011. While Tonic has very big aspirations – to support theatre in the UK to achieve greater gender equality – it is a small company and so we have to make careful choices about where we target our efforts. I spend lots of time looking to identify 'pressure points' – places where, with a bit of work, a great effect can be achieved. For this reason, much of Tonic's work focuses on partnerships with some of the largest theatres in the country, because if they change, others will follow. But it has always been clear to me that youth drama is one of the greatest pressure points of all. It is the engine room of the theatre industry; tomorrow's theatre-makers (not to mention audience members) are to be found today in youth-theatre groups, university drama societies and school drama clubs all over the country. If we can challenge their assumptions about the role of women's stories, voices, and ideas in drama, then change in the profession – in time – will be immeasurably easier to achieve.

Beyond this strategic interest in youth drama, I was convinced that girls were getting a raw deal, and I found that troubling. Having worked previously as a youth-theatre director, I was familiar with the regular challenge of trying to find scripts that had adequate numbers of female roles for all the committed and talented girls that wanted to take part. In nearly all the various youth-drama groups I worked in across a five-year period, there were significantly more girls than boys. However, when it came to finding big-cast, age-appropriate plays for them to work on, I was constantly frustrated by how few there seemed to be that provided enough opportunity for the girls. When looking at contemporary new writing for young actors to perform, one could be mistaken for thinking that youth drama was a predominantly male pursuit, rather than the other way around.

Aside from the practicalities of matching the number of roles to the number of girls in any one drama group, the nature of writing for female characters was something I struggled to get excited about. While there were some notable examples, often the writing for female characters seemed somewhat lacklustre. They tended to be characters at the periphery of the action rather than its heart, with far less to say and do than their male counterparts, and with a tendency towards being one-dimensional, rather than complex or vibrant, funny or surprising. Why was it that in the twenty-first century the *quality* as well as the *quantity* of roles being written for girls still seemed to lag behind those for boys?

Keen to check I wasn't just imagining this imbalance, Tonic conducted a nationwide research study looking into opportunities for girls in youth drama, focusing on the quantity *and* quality of roles available to them. The research was written up into a report, *Swimming in the shallow end*, and is published on the Tonic website. Not only did the research confirm my worst fears; more depressingly, it exceeded them. Many of the research participants were vocal about the social, artistic and emotional benefits that participation in youth-drama productions can have on a young person's life. But so too were they – to quote the report – on 'the erosion to self-esteem, confidence and aspiration when these opportunities are repeatedly held out of reach... [and] for too many girls, this is the case'.

But despite the doom and gloom of the research findings, there remained an exciting proposition; to write stories that weren't currently being put on stage, and to foreground – rather than ignore – the experiences, achievements and world-view of young women, perhaps the group above all others in our society whose situation has altered so dramatically and excitingly over the past hundred or so years. The brief Tonic sets Platform writers is: write a large-cast play specifically for performance by young actors, with mainly or entirely female casts and in which the female characters are no less complex or challenging than the male characters. We ask them to write in such a way that these plays can be performed by young people anywhere in the country, and that there should be scope for every school, college and youth-theatre group performing the play to make a production their own.

There are now seven Platform plays published, of which this is one, and our hope is that there will be many more. Our aspiration – fundraising permitting – is to keep commissioning titles in the series so that over time, Platform will become a new canon of writing for young actors and one that puts girls and their lives centre stage. The first three plays in the series were published in 2015 and have already been performed across the length and breadth of the United Kingdom as well as in Australia, Canada, Hong Kong, Indonesia, Ireland, Luxembourg, Malta and the USA. I look forward to hearing about productions of this play, and a future where great stories about girls and their lives are being staged in theatres, halls, drama studios and classrooms as the rule rather than the exception.

Lucy Kerbel
Director, Tonic

www.tonictheatre-platform.co.uk

Acknowledgements

Tonic would like to thank:

Matt Applewhite, Tamara von Werthern, Jon Barton, Marcelo Dos Santos and all at Nick Hern Books, Moira Buffini, Company Three, Rose Bruford College of Theatre & Performance, the National Youth Theatre of Great Britain, and the National Theatre Studio.

We are grateful to the following for their support of Platform:

The Chapman Charitable Trust, Didymus, Garrick Charitable Trust, Golsoncott Foundation, John Thaw Foundation, and Unity Theatre Trust.

THE GOLSONCOTT FOUNDATION

Tonic was created in 2011 to support the theatre industry to achieve greater gender equality in its workforces and repertoires. Today, Tonic partners with leading theatres and performing-arts organisations around the UK on a range of projects, schemes and creative works. Current and recent partners include the Almeida Theatre, Cast, Chichester Festival Theatre, English Touring Theatre, Headlong, Leeds Playhouse, National Theatre, New Wolsey Theatre, Northern Ballet, Royal Opera House, Royal Shakespeare Company, Sadler's Wells and Sheffield Theatres.

Tonic's approach involves getting to grips with the principles that lie beneath how our industry functions – our working methods, decision-making processes, and organisational structures – and identifying how, in their current form, these can create barriers. Once we have done that, we devise practical yet imaginative alternative approaches and work with our partners to trial and deliver them. Essentially, our goal is to equip our colleagues in UK theatre with the tools they need to ensure more talented women are given the opportunity to rise to the top.

Platform is a collaboration between Tonic and Nick Hern Books. Nick Hern Books also publishes Tonic's books: *100 Great Plays for Women* and *All Change Please: A Practical Guide to Achieving Gender Equality in Theatre*.

www.tonictheatre.co.uk

Tonic have also produced, along with UK Theatre and the Society of London Theatre (SOLT), a theatre casting toolkit to help make the UK's stages and rehearsal rooms more reflective of modern society.

www.tonictheatre.co.uk/work/toolkits-and-resources

Nick Hern Books
Theatre publishers & performing rights agents

We leapt at the chance to publish and license the Platform plays in collaboration with Tonic, and always had high hopes that by making plays available which gave young women the opportunity to take centre stage, we would improve not only their confidence levels, but also start to have a positive effect on the theatrical landscape as a whole.

After all, here at the Performing Rights Department at Nick Hern Books, we're often asked, 'Are there any plays for young people?'... 'Have you got anything for a large cast?'... and 'Is there anything with strong female roles?'

Whilst the answer to these questions is, in each case, a resounding 'Yes!' (and in fact the majority of plays we've published in recent years have been by women), the number of plays that fulfil all three of these criteria – strong roles for a large, predominantly or all-female cast of young actors – has historically been less plentiful. Yet that's where there's so much demand! Nearly every teacher and youth-theatre director in the country knows that it's girls who make up the majority of their casts, and yet the plays available are often dominated by men. Because we can generally only publish what is being produced on the professional stages of the UK, until the theatre industry starts staging more plays with these qualities, the numbers will remain low. It's a vicious circle.

Five years since the first Platform plays were published, I am delighted to report that this circle has somewhat started to disintegrate. It's a source of great pleasure that, aside from their social and political purpose, they're all excellent plays in their own right. As such, we have licensed dozens of productions of the Platform plays to date, providing opportunities and great roles to many hundreds of young women (and young men, for that matter) around the world. While this is cause for celebration, it is no reason for complacency – the journey continues – and we are delighted to publish two great new Platform plays, which will hopefully be received as enthusiastically by schools and youth-theatre groups as the five so far published in the series.

Nick Hern Books looks after the amateur performing rights to well over a thousand plays, and we know from experience that when it comes to choosing the right play it can be confusing (and pricey) to read enough of what's out there until you know which play is right for you. This is why we send out approval copies: up to three plays at a time, for thirty days, after which they have to be paid for, or returned to us in mint condition, and you just need to pay the postage. So there is no reason not to read all of the available Platform plays to see if they will suit your school, college or youth-theatre group. We're very hopeful that one of them will.

Performing rights to all seven Platform plays are available at a specially reduced rate to enable even those on a very tight budget to perform them. Discounts are also available on cast sets of scripts; and the cover images on these books can be supplied, free of charge, for you to use on your poster. If you have any questions about Platform, or any of the plays on our list, or want to talk about what you're looking for, we are always happy to speak with you. Call us on +44 (0)20 8749 4953, or email us at rights@nickhernbooks.co.uk.

And here's to many more Platform plays in the future and to all the young women (and men) bringing them to life!

Tamara von Werthern
Performing Rights Manager
Nick Hern Books

www.nickhernbooks.co.uk/plays-to-perform

Introduction
Beth Flintoff

This is the fourth in a series of historical plays I am lucky enough to have been asked to write in the past couple of years. The experience has made me realise how profoundly dissatisfied I am with the way history has been presented to us so far, and how happy to discover that all along there have been countless stories of remarkable women, sitting unnoticed in the dustbin of history, waiting for someone to brush them off. This story, of a group of women forced to spend years closed up together and trying not to go mad in the process, was one such forgotten tale of courage and ingenuity that deserves to be told.

If such a thing as a completely accurate historical play exists, this isn't it. I did a lot of research, spending many days poring over books in libraries, but then compressed, ignored, and bullied the facts into the shape of a drama. I have stayed true to the essential story, and, more importantly, I tried to work my way into the heads of these women, to respect their stories through the prism of the centuries. The one total invention is the character of Rose. It's hard to relate to the actions of the fabulously rich and/or royal unless you're in that top one per cent yourself, so I wanted to look at the story through the eyes of someone more ordinary. I wanted Rose to take us into Tutbury, with her eyes open wide and her jaw on the floor, gasping in disbelief at the way the other half lives.

Below I have tried to place the characters of Elizabeth, Bess and Mary in some kind of historical context. All the other characters at least began their lives in the history books, though Cecily is literally just a name on a list. I have no proof whatsoever that she spied for Walsingham, but he certainly did have female spies. In the name of economy I have laced together Walsingham's role in the history with that of another adviser, William Cecil. In fact, Cecil was the senior official and would have been more likely to give Elizabeth advice, while Walsingham would have been out in the field collecting information. It's true that Elizabeth had smallpox scars, that her half-sister Queen Mary ate marmalade to aid her fertility, and that at this point Elizabeth was under relentless pressure to marry. It's true that Seaton and Livingston stayed with Mary until she died; Livingston's husband lived in the household with them, but Seaton never married. And it's true that Mary's cushion cover to Norfolk was delivered by a man called Borthwick, who then disappeared and could not be traced. This was a point I worked backwards from, to get to Rose.

Being asked to write a play designed to be performed primarily by young women is an honour and a privilege. I spent seven years working with the Senior Youth Theatre at The Watermill Theatre in Newbury, so I understand the difficulty of finding plays that do not result in a bunfight for sparse female roles. I know what it's like to be that director, but I also know what it's like to be in that cast. It feels like only yesterday that I couldn't have a speaking role in the school play because there was only one female part and I'd had a go last year. Tonic represents a movement for change that I am thrilled to be a part of. Every performance by a youth or community theatre is a miracle, a triumph of hard work and faith over practical and financial obstacles. It's a source of great pride for a playwright to be a breeze-block in the building of such miracles. I hope you have a whole world of fun doing it.

Acknowledgements

I am so grateful to Lucy Kerbel at Tonic Theatre for asking me to write this play, and for her intelligent and insightful dramaturgy; to Liz and Harland Walshaw for telling me about the Oxburgh Hangings; to Ade Morris and Hedda Beeby at The Watermill for suggesting I was a writer before I had worked it out for myself; to Nicola Gentle for help with embroidery techniques; to Ola Ince for her directorial suggestions; to the cast, David Zoob and the whole team at Rose Bruford College. I am thankful for the existence of libraries in general, specifically Reading University Library and the Bodleian Library in Oxford.

I am grateful to my father, Nick, who bought me history books as a child, and my mother, Jane, whose fascination with grammar and words makes her a great proofreader, and endlessly indebted to my husband, Nick, who is just very nice about it all.

Finally, I wish to pay tribute to Gypsy the cat, who solemnly scrutinised every word in the first draft, but sadly did not live to throw up all over the final version. She was my constant writing companion and I feel her absence very much.

B.F.

Historical Context

In February 1569, Mary, Queen of Scots arrived at Tutbury
Castle, having escaped in a fishing boat from the land she had
once ruled, with her reputation in tatters. As Queen Elizabeth I's
cousin, she was potentially the next in line to the English
throne, making her very presence in England a threat. She also
had a son, at a time when Elizabeth's apparent reluctance to
choose a husband and sort out a suitable heir for herself was
seen as deeply disturbing by most people in England. Unsure of
what to do with her cousin, Elizabeth charged her friends, the
Earl and Countess of Shrewsbury, with Mary's care, while her
previous conduct was investigated. It was meant to be a brief
stay, but the years dragged by, and Mary became the subject of
endless plots and intrigues until she was finally executed in
1587.

Mary, Queen of Scots

Mary's problems in Scotland stemmed from the accusation that
she was involved in the murder of her second husband, Lord
Darnley. Their relationship had been stormy; Darnley demanded
to be named co-sovereign and Mary refused. He was jealous of
Mary's secretary, David Rizzio, and had him murdered in front
of her eyes during dinner, while she was six months pregnant.
Divorce was discussed, but didn't happen, and it seemed for a
few months as though Mary was trying to reconcile with him.
But in February 1567, Darnley died from a deliberately caused
explosion in Edinburgh while Mary was attending a friend's
wedding. The man everyone thought behind the murder, the
Earl of Bothwell, was one of her friends. A few weeks later,
Mary went to visit her baby son in Stirling and on the way back
was met by Bothwell and taken, either willingly or by force, to
his castle. Bothwell had himself been divorced twelve days

earlier. Shortly afterwards she announced that they were married, and that she was pregnant with twins. To this day it is not clear whether Mary wanted to marry him or not; it is possible that she didn't want to say she had been forced because she was afraid she would disinherit the babies.

Mary's marriage to Bothwell was deeply unpopular, suspected as he was of murdering Darnley. Twenty-six Scottish lords banded together and raised an army, and in the ensuing battle Mary was taken prisoner, carried through Edinburgh in front of a jeering crowd, and then taken to a fortified island. There she miscarried her twins and was forced to abdicate in favour of her one-year-old son, James VI of Scotland (later also James I of England). Her half-brother Moray was made Regent, and Bothwell was driven into exile in Denmark where he went insane. The following year she managed to escape, arriving in England by fishing boat. She was taken first to Bolton, then to Tutbury Castle, and into the care of Bess and George Shrewsbury, in February 1569. Tutbury was a depressing place by all accounts – cold, damp and small – so in the end Mary was moved to other houses owned by the Shrewsburys, shunted from place to place at great expense, depending on the state of her health and Queen Elizabeth's commands.

The Oxburgh Hangings

The Oxburgh Hangings are a remarkable collection of needlework hangings kept at Oxburgh Hall, a National Trust property in Norfolk. The embroideries were made by Mary, Bess and their ladies during the long term of imprisonment. In the stifling atmosphere of her incarceration, Mary used embroidery as a form of therapy and communication with the outside world, when more conventional means were forbidden. The most famous of the embroideries is now known as the Norfolk Panel; it shows a giant female hand pruning an orchard. It was a coded message to the Duke of Norfolk that he should marry her and bring an end to Elizabeth's barren, childless reign. Marriage was a way out for Mary: a means of restoring her to the throne and escaping her imprisonment. For Norfolk, it represented an opportunity to scale the unimaginable heights of becoming a royal. Elizabeth repeatedly asked him if he was considering marriage to Mary, and he denied it, until the story came out that the marriage was planned alongside a rebellion in the north of England. Norfolk was arrested, then released, but a year later he was still plotting along the same lines. During his trial, the embroidery and other incriminating letters from Mary were used as evidence against him. He was found guilty of treason and executed.

After 450 years, the colour has faded, but the hangings are still astonishing. I made the trip to Norfolk in the early stages of my research, and it completely changed the play. The small room containing the hangings gives a sense of who these women were, and the appalling claustrophobia of their situation. There's an obsession with journeys, with the outside world and with exotic animals that they would never have the freedom to see. Flora, fauna, birds and beasts are all represented, from an ordinary chicken through to monstrous, nightmare-like inventions, full of rage and impotent fury. Flowers burst out of the borders; emblems of births, deaths, the inevitability of an enclosed life. Day after day in the same rooms, doing nothing. 'Who am I?' 'Where are we?' 'Why are we here?' they seem to ask.

Bess of Hardwick

Bess's embroidery is known as the Cavendish Hanging, because it refers not to her fourth husband, or even her third, but her second. From humble beginnings, Bess had used her intelligence, financial ability and charm to accumulate vast wealth. Her first husband died very early in their marriage, while they were both still teenagers, so her second, William Cavendish, probably felt like her first real relationship. The couple were together for ten years and had eight children. Together they built Chatsworth, an enormous house in Derbyshire, but then he died suddenly. The debts he left behind meant she was forced to marry again immediately, and when her third husband, William St Loe, also died, she again remarried with speed, and this time in a spectacular raising of her status, to the Earl of Shrewsbury. Her fourth marriage made her the richest woman in England apart from the Queen.

William Cavendish kept a detailed, tidy journal, and it seems he taught Bess how to keep accounts. The Accounts Room at Hardwick Hall is a real thing: an extraordinary room that looks like the Tudor equivalent of a giant filing cabinet gone mad. Boxes line the walls up to the ceiling. The room would have been built after Cavendish's death, and I had a vision of Bess hiding away behind her accounts when her problems oppressed her. The Cavendish Hanging is a devastating expression of grief: in Bess's world, the rain is in the shape of tears, and the Latin motto reads 'Tears witness that the quenched flame lives.' It was only after leaving Oxburgh that I noticed the glove in the bottom left-hand corner, ripped in two. It seemed like a perfect metaphor for the relationship between Bess and Rose.

At first her fourth marriage was a success – the Earl's letters to her from Court are full of love and affection. But the strain of guarding a royal prisoner for years took a terrible toll. Bess accused George of having an affair with Mary; he accused her of spending too much money, and they both found looking after a queen stressful, expensive and thankless. Elizabeth did not like having to pay the expenses, so they had to often pay for things themselves. Eventually the couple separated and the Earl's letters became bitter and angry.

Hardwick Hall, near Chesterfield, is where Bess lived both as a child and later as an older, much richer woman, when she rebuilt the Hall in spectacular fashion. It's an extraordinary building: an outrageous, angry display of wealth after she became estranged from George. The building glares down at you as you drive up the M1, Bess's initials (ES) displayed in giant lettering on the ramparts. The Zenobia and Penelope tapestries are part of a series displayed here: larger-than-life, sleekly black and gold, they are breathtakingly modern in themselves. These are images of strong women, tall and fierce, without an ounce of religious imagery or the usual pious celebrations of the status quo. Bess obviously loved the Penelope story; she had an entire room with a throne at one end and little else apart from wall-to-wall tapestries telling the story of Odysseus returning home. The concept of women quietly stitching in submissive, elegant silence, does not apply at Hardwick Hall. It's more like a proud display of female fierceness, well before its time.

Production Note

Casting

The play can be performed by a minimum of sixteen people (twelve female, four male), with no maximum size. I have deliberately kept the number of waiting ladies flexible to help with differing cast sizes. I think you would struggle to have only one waiting lady, but should that happen, feel free to change 'we' to 'I', etc. If, like me, you prefer actors to have named roles, there are plenty to choose from, including Blanche Parry, Katherine 'Kat' Ashley, Elizabeth Knollys, Lettice Knollys, Mary Radcliffe and Mary Sidney. They would have generally had the title 'Lady X'. If you are short of men, Huntingdon's role in the penultimate scene could be performed by Lord Walsingham, with the name reference changed accordingly.

Narrators

When we were rehearsing the play at Rose Bruford College, the 'split' characters (Bess 1 and 2, Rose 1 and 2, Mary 1 and 2) were the most successful when they had a close physical connection to each other, rather than staying separately to one side talking to the audience. Rose 2 says what Rose 1 is thinking, so she needs to be feeling the same feelings, experiencing the same events, and their energy should mirror each other.

Accents

The play contains characters speaking in a whole host of different ways, but there is no need to try to find any 'truth' in the accents unless you wish to. George, Bess and Cecily grew up in Derbyshire; Rose in Staffordshire; Mary, Seaton and Livingston may have had either French or Scottish accents because they spent their childhoods in France; Elizabeth and Walsingham would probably have spoken with something approaching what we now call RP (received pronunciation); while Norfolk could have had either an RP or Norfolk accent. Rose's speech rhythms are deliberately relaxed to give the sense that she has grown up in a different social circle to the others; but beyond that, if you prefer, feel free to use the natural accents of the cast.

Set and Costumes

The intention is that you can perform this play with minimal set and costumes, or go all out and have the full Elizabethan extravaganza – whichever you choose. The only person who really needs to look in a particular way is Elizabeth, because her image was an enforced part of her identity, something she could not escape from. But how you show that is up to you. The scenes should generally flow smoothly from one to the next, with minimal gaps.

A Note on the Text

… indicates that a character has run out of things to say.

– indicates an interruption.

/ indicates the point of interruption during the previous character's speech.

THE GLOVE THIEF

Characters

Three of the characters – ROSE, MARY *and* BESS *– have their own narrator. The narrator is given the number '2' after her name.*

THE SHREWSBURY HOUSEHOLD

BESS (1 *and* 2), *Countess of Shrewsbury; 'Bess of Hardwick', one of the richest women in England, after Queen Elizabeth I*

ROSE (1 *and* 2), *a young woman who has grown up in Tutbury, Staffordshire*

GEORGE TALBOT, *Earl of Shrewsbury; Bess's fourth husband*

CECILY, *a servant working for the Shrewsbury household*

OTHER SERVANTS

QUEEN MARY'S HOUSEHOLD

MARY (1 *and* 2), *the former queen of Scotland, who has abdicated her throne and fled the country to England*

MARY SEATON, *a lady-in-waiting to Mary, Queen of Scots, who has been with her since she was a child*

MARY LIVINGSTON, *a lady-in-waiting to Mary, Queen of Scots, who has also been with her since she was a child*

JOHN LESLEY, *Bishop of Ross, Mary's ambassador to Queen Elizabeth*

QUEEN ELIZABETH'S HOUSEHOLD

ELIZABETH I, QUEEN OF ENGLAND, *Queen for the last ten years; the daughter of Henry VIII and Anne Boleyn*

LADY PARRY, *a lady-in-waiting to Queen Elizabeth, who has been with her for many years*

THOMAS, *Duke of Norfolk, a nobleman who had once been close to Elizabeth; one of the richest men in England*

LORD WALSINGHAM, *an adviser to Queen Elizabeth*

WAITING LADIES TO QUEEN ELIZABETH, *women who attend the Queen at all times of the day and night*

COURTIERS AND GUARDS

OTHERS

THE EARL OF HUNTINGDON, *an English nobleman*

VILLAGERS OF TUTBURY

4

ACT ONE

Scene One

Tutbury, February 1569.

ROSE 1 *and* ROSE 2.

ROSE 2. The night before it all starts, I have a row with Ma because she's found out I've been stealing. She yells at me, says I could have got caught. I tell her –

ROSE 1. I never stole anything in me life!

ROSE 2. Which is a lie – I steal something at least once a week. Ma does her usual bit about how she wishes she had a son instead of me, that she can't hold her head high in society –

ROSE 1. What are you talking about? We live in a stinking hovel!

ROSE 2. She gasps and takes a swing – but it doesn't hurt because she's too drunk and can't see what she's doing. Then Ma's New Man comes in.

ROSE 1. Oh, no...

ROSE 2. Incidentally he does have a name, but they change so often I just call them all New Man. Ma says, 'Oh, New Man, she's been stealing again.' And New Man says, 'We're not angry, just disappointed.'

So I leave before being tempted to throw something very hard at his face.

I go to The Dog and Partridge. I drink the dregs of someone else's pint while they're not looking, and relieve a poor old gent of a burden he shouldn't have to shoulder in his later years.

ROSE 1 *holds out a wallet.*

And then I go to my favourite place, which is this ditch on the other side of the river, just beyond the village.

ROSE 1 *sits on the floor.*

I don't sleep very much because it's February and I'm gonna die if I don't keep moving, but for a while I wrap myself up and look at the castle. It's high above my head, and I can see the candlelight flickering where the rich folks go about from room to room. I reckon they've got time to have clever thoughts because they don't have to think about how they're gonna survive the night.

I tell myself:

ROSE 1. Tomorrow, I'm gonna finally leave this place. I can't stay in Tutbury. I've got to get out of here, go and learn to do something proper and beautiful, like... sewing!

ROSE 2. Don't laugh. I know it's not for people like me. But I like patterns. These grubby little hands that currently steal from others could become –

ROSE 1. The delicate fingers of a seamstress!

ROSE 2. Alright. It's a long shot.

But the wallet I've stolen will give me enough money to get to a new village, get employment somewhere, start doing something with my life.

It feels good.

ROSE 1. Tomorrow is the start of a new dawn!

ROSE 2. Then I open up the wallet.

ROSE 1 *opens the wallet.*

And there's nothing in it.

ROSE 1 *sighs. She puts her head in her hands.*

And I wonder how long I can just sit there, without moving, considering the sheer, blinding, pointlessness of my life, before I freeze into a statue.

But that's because it's the night *before* it starts, and as of tomorrow, I start to be a little bit less pointless.

This is the story of a thief who changed the course of history.

Enter BESS 2, *a* WAITING LADY, *and* MARY 2.

MARY 2. No. It's the story of a queen who triumphs over adversity.

WAITING LADY. It's the story of a sovereign who extends the hand of friendship to an unworthy cousin.

BESS 2. It's an administrative nightmare, that's what it is.

Everyone exits except BESS 2, *who stays onstage for the next scene.*

Scene Two

In The Dog and Partridge Inn, Tutbury, the next day.

BESS 1, BESS 2 *and* WALSINGHAM.

BESS 2. I am not fond of taverns, especially the notorious Dog and Partridge. But I have been summoned here to meet the master schemer himself, Lord Walsingham. And an invitation from Walsingham cannot be refused.

BESS 1 *is looking at paperwork.*

I am reading papers that chart the journey of Mary, Queen of the Scots, as she makes her inexorable way towards my house.

WALSINGHAM. She escaped from Scotland in a fishing boat and has been held at Bolton Castle. She will arrive here tomorrow.

BESS 1. Why us?

WALSINGHAM. If she goes home now, her own people will kill her. But if she travels to France or Spain she will become a rallying cry for Catholics everywhere. The kingdom is too unstable – there are plots and rumours enough already without adding fuel to the fire. Her Majesty feels that you are one of the few people she can trust. Mary will stay with you until a safe return to Scotland can be arranged.

BESS 1. We are barely ready. The castle is freezing and the kitchen's too small.

WALSINGHAM. Her Majesty appreciates the inconvenience.

BESS 1. We will need more money.

WALSINGHAM. Your husband indicated otherwise.

BESS 1. George knows nothing of the accounts.

WALSINGHAM. We have already provided a / significant –

BESS 1. Nothing like enough – it will cost me fifty-two pounds a week.

WALSINGHAM. I will entreat Her Majesty for more funds.

BESS 1. Thank you.

WALSINGHAM. Grant me a favour in return. I need to know everything she says. Obtain a copy of all correspondence and send it to me.

BESS 1. I thought she was forbidden to write –

WALSINGHAM. On the contrary, it should be encouraged. How else will we know her plans? But she must not know it is being intercepted. One of my men will come here once a week to collect anything you have. If there is something urgent – concerning Her Majesty's safety – it is better for it to come straight to London. Send someone who would never be suspected.

BESS 1 goes to the door.

BESS 1. Cecily.

Enter CECILY.

CECILY. Yes, madam?

BESS 1. She's been with me since she was a little girl. (*To* CECILY.) This is Lord Walsingham.

WALSINGHAM (*studying* CECILY). Yes. Good.

BESS 1. How will I make sure she reaches you safely?

WALSINGHAM. I have people stationed at inns all the way along the London road – if she presents an agreed token she will be looked after and accompanied to the next one with no questions asked. What will be the token?

BESS 1. This ring?

She shows him a ring, which he briefly inspects.

WALSINGHAM. Very well.

BESS 1. We have insufficient staff.

WALSINGHAM. Recruit more, pick them up off the street if you have to.

BESS 1. I cannot just coopt people –

WALSINGHAM. Accuse them of a crime, then tell them they can either face justice or come and work for you.

BESS 1. Is that how you do it?

WALSINGHAM. Cecily, here is your first task. See that girl out there? I want you to make it look as though she has stolen your mistress's glove.

CECILY is alarmed. She looks at BESS 1, who takes off her glove and gives it to her.

CECILY. Madam – I –

WALSINGHAM goes to the window and shouts –

WALSINGHAM. Stop – thief! That girl stole the lady's glove! Catch her!

(*Back to CECILY and BESS 1.*) You've got about a minute before they start to pull her hair out. (*To CECILY.*) When she's on the floor, plant the glove.

BESS 1. Go.

CECILY exits.

WALSINGHAM. Plenty of time for a drink before you face the cold air.

He pours them both a glass of wine.

How you stand living in the north I have no idea.

BESS 1. We are born with thicker skins.

They drink.

BESS 2. I consider my life up until this point. I try to dislodge the feeling of dread that sits in my stomach.

WALSINGHAM. I understand that the task is a daunting one.

BESS 1. Not at all.

WALSINGHAM. Queen Elizabeth is counting on you.

BESS 1. She has relied upon me before.

WALSINGHAM. I hear that you were great friends, as girls?

BESS 1. Yes.

WALSINGHAM. It is wonderful that out of a calamity such as this, the relationship between two old friends can be rekindled.

BESS 2. Why do I fear this, quite so much?

BESS 1. It is.

They drink again.

BESS 2. I wonder if that girl outside is still alive. How can he be so casual? I will count to ten in my head, then excuse myself.

One, two, three –

BESS 1. Please, excuse me, my lord. I should rescue my new recruit.

BESS 1 *and* BESS 2 *exit.*

After a moment, WALSINGHAM *exits in a different direction.*

Scene Three

Outside The Dog and Partridge Inn.

ROSE 1 *and* ROSE 2 *are there amongst a crowd of* VILLAGERS.

ROSE 2. So, the next day is *epically* freezing, and I head towards The Dog and Partridge. When this bloke from inside the pub yells out of the window that I stole some woman's glove.

ROSE 1. What? Me?

The VILLAGERS *surround her, threatening.*

VILLAGER. Did you?

ROSE 1. No, I didn't!

VILLAGER. I bet she did.

VILLAGER. Vicious child!

VILLAGER. Gloves are precious!

VILLAGER. Chop her hands off!

ROSE 2. The people of Tutbury hold somewhat *conservative* views on criminal justice.

Enter CECILY.

VILLAGER. Turn out your pockets.

ROSE 1. Look. I didn't do a thing. I'm just gonna back off, here, and go back to minding me own business.

She backs into CECILY, *who catches her.*

VILLAGER. You're not going anywhere!

CECILY *pretends to feel in* ROSE 1*'s pocket, and brings out* BESS 1*'s glove. She holds it up.*

CECILY. This is the glove she stole! She's a thief!

The VILLAGERS *roar their fury. They start to push* ROSE 1 *about a bit.*

ROSE 1. Get off!

VILLAGER. We don't want the likes of you 'ere!

VILLAGER. Put 'er in the stocks!

VILLAGER. She should be hanged and burning in hell!

The crowd becomes violent. ROSE 1 *is on the floor. Someone kneels beside her and starts bashing her head against the floor. The* VILLAGERS *egg each other on. The beating is vicious.*

ROSE 2. Now, ladies and gents, don't panic, this is the worst bit, I promise. The rest of this story is gonna be – trust me – glorious.

Cos then, this happened.

Enter BESS 1.

BESS 1. Stop it.

Pause. BESS 1 *has a powerful presence. The* VILLAGERS *fall silent. Just the sound of* ROSE 1, *crying.*

BESS 1 *studies* ROSE 1 *for a moment. Then she looks around the ensemble.*

It is my glove, I will deal with her.

The VILLAGERS *filter off, disappointed that the show has come to an end.*

Cecily.

CECILY *helps* ROSE 1 *to her feet. She is dazed, confused, mumbling.*

What is your name?

ROSE 1. Rose. Miss…

CECILY. My lady.

ROSE 1. Lady…

BESS 1. How old are you, Rose?

ROSE 1. I dunno…

BESS 1. Nineteen, twenty?

ROSE 1. Yeah.

BESS 1. I'm sorry that you were hurt. We will take care of you now.

BESS 1 *starts to go.*

ROSE 1. Wha– where we going?

CECILY. To the castle –

ROSE 1. I ain't going in no dungeons – I got rights –

BESS 1. No – you will work for me.

ROSE 1. Well, what if I don't want to – this is kidnap. (*Feebly*.) Help! Enforced slavery!

CECILY. Would you prefer to stay here and be put in the stocks?

ROSE 1. No, but –

BESS 1 *goes to her – with a sudden intensity –*

BESS 1. Why were you standing on the street, Rose? Do you have anywhere else to go? A loving family, a husband?

Beat. ROSE 1 *is defiant, angry, confused.*

ROSE 1. Not 'zactly.

BESS 1 *reaches out her hand. Tenderly, she touches* ROSE 1*'s cheek.*

BESS 1. Then, please, come and work for me. You will be safe – warmer. Not so hungry.

ROSE 1 *nods.*

Will you promise not to steal from me?

ROSE 1. Yeah.

BESS 1. Thank you.

BESS 1 *exits.*

ROSE 1. Who is that?

CECILY. Don't you recognise Lady Shrewsbury?

ROSE 1 *doesn't.*

Bess of Hardwick?

The former Lady Cavendish?

ROSE 1. How many names does one woman need?

CECILY. It's as if you've been living under a rock.

ROSE 1. Sort of rocky ditch. Why's she want me?

CECILY. She's looking for staff whose loyalty she can absolutely depend on.

(*Studying* ROSE 1 *grimly*.) We've had to plumb new depths.
Come on.

CECILY *helps* ROSE 1 *offstage*.

ROSE 2 *looks at the audience*.

She beams.

ROSE 2. Brilliant, right? That's how it started. Just like that.

Scene Four

An inn on the road from Bolton to Tutbury.

MARY 1 *is completely still*. MARY 2 *is watching*.

SEATON *and* LIVINGSTON, *her ladies-in-waiting, are gazing at* MARY 1 *in equally motionless, adoring silence*.

MARY 2. I am remaining completely still, to give the illusion of calm. Later they will say I was like marble for hours at a time, and I like that. I shall become a legend. After all, a queen is history.

Inside my head is chatter as I consider options. I have survived an abduction, assassination attempt, double miscarriage, and three bad husbands, so this is not the worst. I have escaped Scotland. I am safe now.

Sometimes a memory – a past wrong, a death, a baby left behind – advances like an army towards my heart.

LIVINGSTON. What can we get for you, Your Grace?

Still MARY 1 *does not move*.

MARY 2. But I am strong. I will not dwell on vintage deeds. Amongst the flowers of my enemy there is always a weed. I will find the weed and nurture it until it chokes the garden.

(To MARY 1.) It's time.

MARY 1 *makes a slight movement: the stillness is over. The women immediately are geared to action, they have seen all this before.* SEATON *moves forward to* MARY 1 *with a glass of wine, which she takes.*

I tidy out my brain with a list.

MARY 1. What do we have?

SEATON. People?

MARY 1. Yes.

SEATON. Secretary, household steward, surgeon, apothecary, clerk, doctor, cook. Other secretaries, ordinary servants. Thirty-one in total.

MARY 2. Thirty-one people on the list.

MARY 1. She will try to reduce our numbers.

SEATON. Reduce us?

MARY 1. Elizabeth will never pay for all of this. What about my things?

LIVINGSTON. The books, most of the linen –

MARY 1. Not all?

LIVINGSTON. One cart was tumbled on the road. But it will catch up.

MARY 1. Gowns?

LIVINGSTON. Three good. Two for everyday.

MARY 1. Send for more.

LIVINGSTON. Very well, Your Grace.

MARY 1. I cannot let their eyes be disappointed.

MARY 2. Looks. Youth. *Beauty.* They go on the list.

A sharp pain in the side of MARY 1*'s stomach.* MARY 1 *gasps.*

LIVINGSTON. Your Grace?

She holds up a hand to forbid more talking. They surround her anxiously.

MARY 2. It is months since the loss of my twins, but the pain lingers on. And pain, in private, is no use, because I need them all to see the glory of my courage. But public pain, witnessed by, say, a sympathetic man. That will be of use. Pain goes on the list.

SEATON. What can we do?

MARY 1. Talk to me of good things.

Pause.

MARY 2. The silence is dangerous. Please think of something!

SEATON. You will go walking in the spring amongst the orchids.

Relief.

LIVINGSTON (*inspired*). Yes – and we will get a falconer!

MARY 1. A falconer…

SEATON. And then… you will write letters to all your friends, and they will reassure you of their support.

They tend to her – biscuits and wine and a poultice for her brow.

MARY 2. I love these women like their bones are my bones. They find the joy in this stupid blinkered world amongst these raw and heathen people. When they close their eyes I swear they see hyacinths.

When I close my eyes, I see blood.

It's why I am a queen and they are not. I see the death and terror and I ride towards it. My body is prepared. My blood is royal.

Blood goes on the list.

Enter JOHN LESLEY, the Bishop of Ross, and GEORGE TALBOT, the Earl of Shrewsbury. They bow respectfully.

This is it.

MARY 1. Good morning, John.

LESLEY. Your Grace, may I introduce the Earl of Shrewsbury? He is here to escort us to Tutbury Castle.

GEORGE. Your Grace.

He draws himself up for his speech, very formal.

On behalf of Her Majesty, Queen Elizabeth I, I bid you welcome to England. She is full of sympathy for the way you have been treated by the Scottish people.

MARY 1. Thank you.

GEORGE. From now on you will be under the care of myself and my wife, Bess, at Tutbury Castle. We will make you as comfortable as we can.

MARY 2. Find the weed. Nurture it.

MARY 1. My Lord Shrewsbury. I am so relieved to have reached a safe haven at last.

GEORGE. You will be well looked after in Tutbury.

MARY 1. What a terrible burden it must be for you and your charming wife. I will do my best to be a pleasing house guest.

GEORGE (*relaxing a little*). Your Grace, our task is not a burden, but a source of immense pride.

MARY 1. If nothing else can come out of this terrible business, I pray that we will become friends.

GEORGE. Indeed, Madam, I hope so too.

They exit.

Scene Five

Tutbury Castle. ROSE 2, ROSE 1 *and* CECILY.

ROSE 1 *is wearing a new dress.*

ROSE 2. Before I know it, I'm standing in Tutbury Castle and no one's trying to arrest me, and I'm wearing some amazing dress thing that I pretend to think is stupid –

ROSE 1. This is stupid.

ROSE 2. But actually is amazing – and she says:

CECILY. We've got to make you look proper, she's coming any minute.

ROSE 1. Who?

CECILY. The Queen.

ROSE 1 *is aghast. She starts to hyperventilate.*

Not *our* queen, the other one. Mary of Scotland.

ROSE 1. Wha… I dunno what to say to a ruddy queen!

CECILY. Don't say anything at all.

ROSE 1. But what if she asks me something? I can't just stand there like a donkey –

CECILY. Reply in as few words as possible, with your head bowed.

ROSE 1. Head bowed, yeah – that's good – you're good. You've done this before.

CECILY. And at the end of everything, say 'Your Majesty.'

ROSE 1. Your Majesty.

CECILY. Or 'Your Grace' – or –

ROSE 1. 'Your *Beauteousness*' –

CECILY. No, don't say that.

ROSE 1. Sorry.

ROSE 2. She takes me through the castle, along narrow passages, past chambers where maids are hanging things on the walls, past a pantry and a kitchen bigger than our house, and I'm trying to act like I've seen it all before. But really I'm panicking because I can't speak how they all do, and in my head I'm saying proper, grown up stuff, like –

ROSE 1 (*posh voice*). I shall never forget your kindness.

ROSE 2. But instead what comes out is –

ROSE 1. What in the name of holy pigeon crap is *that*?

ROSE 2. Because in front of us is a tapestry of a woman holding a spear that's the height of a house.

ROSE 1. Look at it! Just look at it. She is armed and dangerous!

She goes to touch it, stroking her finger along the stitching.

Enter BESS 1.

CECILY. Don't touch that!

BESS 1. Zenobia. Queen of Palmyra. Do you like it?

ROSE 1. Who did it?

BESS 1. At Chatsworth I have a personal embroiderer – he assisted me, with one or two apprentices.

ROSE 1. Is this thread made out of gold?

BESS 1. Gold silk. It is not so much. The Countess of Salisbury spent fourteen thousand pounds on hangings around her bed when she was about to give birth.

ROSE 1. *Why?*

BESS 1. She knew the room would be full of guests afterwards.

ROSE 1. I've never seen a woman stand like that before. It's like she doesn't care.

BESS 1. Perhaps she doesn't.

ROSE 1. What's she gone and put herself in armour for?

BESS 1. You tell me.

ROSE 1. I dunno –

BESS 1. What do you see?

ROSE 1. Um. (*Uncertainly, she studies the embroidery.*) Her dress. It's moving.

BESS 1. Yes – why?

ROSE 1. Cos she's on her way out, to sort stuff.

BESS 1. What else?

ROSE 1. Well… that spear is in front of the arch, so she's walking through it. (*With growing confidence.*) And she's afraid, that's why she's reaching for the helmet – the people out there have bows and arrows and they don't care about hurting her – so she's terrified, but she's gonna do it anyway.

BESS 1. Very good!

ROSE 1. But why's she wearing those red shoes? I'd have given her a proper pair of boots. Maybe the shoes represent the blood she's gonna shed? Or her own blood? Or guilt over blood she's shed in the past? We need more information on the shoes.

Beat.

CECILY. You are *really* odd.

A bell rings.

BESS 1. She is here.

SERVANTS rush in, smoothing their clothes and getting ready to receive the royal guest.

Enter (ideally up an aisle or through the auditorium) MARY 1 with GEORGE, LESLEY, MARY LIVINGSTON, and MARY SEATON.

BESS 1 and all her SERVANTS, including ROSE 1, kneel.

Pause.

GEORGE. Your Grace, may I present my wife, Bess?

MARY 1. Lady Shrewsbury, how delightful to meet at last. I have heard so much about you from your charming husband on the journey.

BESS 1. I bid you welcome, Your Grace. We have the rooms warmed and aired.

SEATON. She needs to rest –

BESS 1. Of course –

SEATON. – and then eat.

BESS 1. We have supper ready –

SEATON. Nothing too rich. She has not been well on the journey.

BESS 1. My servants will show Your Grace upstairs.

MARY 1. Thank you – ah, Shrewsbury!

She leans on him, delicate, and tender, like a flower. It's very convincing.

How you have saved me from despair on this journey with your gentle spirit. Now at least you will be spared my constant company.

GEORGE. It has been a pleasure, Your Grace.

One of the SERVANTS *leads the way offstage, followed by* MARY 1, SEATON *and* LIVINGSTON.

BESS 1. You all know your duties. Thank you.

The rest of the SERVANTS *exit, including* ROSE 1.

BESS 1 *turns to* GEORGE.

How many are there?

GEORGE. Thirty-one.

BESS 1. We do not have enough space.

GEORGE. I could write to Her Majesty and ask for her to be moved to Chatsworth.

BESS 1. No – wait. They will be crowded and uncomfortable here. Some are sure to leave of their own accord.

GEORGE. Walsingham says she is not to leave the house. But I have a separate letter from Her Majesty saying she may go riding as she loves the exercise.

BESS 1. We cannot follow both commands.

GEORGE. Which do we choose?

BESS 1. For now, we should obey the instructions of the Queen. You can ride with her, you are a good horseman, and make sure she comes to no harm.

GEORGE. I have missed you.

He holds out his hand to her. She doesn't take it.

BESS 1. There is so much to do.

She exits. GEORGE, *rejected, is left standing alone.*

Scene Six

Whitehall Palace, London.

The WAITING LADIES *talk to the audience.*

WAITING LADY. People say she's not a morning person –

WAITING LADY. But that's because she works for half the night –

WAITING LADY. And it takes time to get her ready.

WAITING LADY. No one may see her before she is properly dressed –

WAITING LADY. Apart from us.

WAITING LADY. The life of a queen may appear charming but it is full of a thousand frustrations and fears.

WAITING LADY. The demands on her are very great.

WAITING LADY. Out there, the courtiers and the nobles and the very high men –

WAITING LADY. They need her to be everything:

WAITING LADY. Confident, yet humble –

WAITING LADY. Intelligent, yet seek their advice –

WAITING LADY. Oh, how they love to give advice! –

WAITING LADY. She must seem young and beautiful, no matter her age or natural appearance.

WAITING LADY. She is often told she is in danger –

WAITING LADY. Poison, treachery, insubordination, rebellion –

WAITING LADY. They tell her: all these things are just around the corner.

WAITING LADY. Only recently the locks on all the doors were changed, just in case.

WAITING LADY. So, sometimes, when she needs to think, she paces up and down this gallery with as few attendants as possible.

Enter WALSINGHAM.

WALSINGHAM. God save the Queen.

WAITING LADIES (*murmuring*). God save the Queen.

WALSINGHAM. How is your mistress this morning?

WAITING LADY. She slept deeply at first, then more fitfully at dawn, my lord.

WALSINGHAM. Did she eat before bed?

WAITING LADY. A light snack, my Lord.

WALSINGHAM. Meat, or fish?

WAITING LADY. Fish.

WALSINGHAM. Her cycle – is it regular now? Have her courses come?

WAITING LADY. She has not asked for her black girdle yet, my lord – she usually does when her bleeding starts.

WALSINGHAM. Perhaps she should have a hot bath.

WAITING LADY. Yes, my lord.

Enter THOMAS, *very bouncy*.

THOMAS. To the beauteous Ladies of the Bedchamber, I wish you a good morning!

WAITING LADY. My Lord Duke – the Queen is not expecting you today –

THOMAS. Indeed not – I am a pleasant surprise!

WAITING LADY. But she specifically instructed –

THOMAS. I do not need a special invitation to visit my *cousin*.

WALSINGHAM. I beg your pardon, my lord. You do.

THOMAS. Oh. Walsingham. There you are. I see that you do not wait for an invitation.

WALSINGHAM. My lord, I do not merit invitation; I merely follow instructions.

THOMAS. Is it true that one of the Gentlemen Ushers of the Privy Chamber has been awarded a castle in Hampshire worth one hundred pounds a year?

WALSINGHAM. I would not know, my lord.

THOMAS. He's a glorified doorkeeper! She never gives me anything.

WALSINGHAM. Perhaps she feels you do not need it.

THOMAS. Well – the thought would be nice!

WAITING LADY. She comes!

A WAITING LADY *throws rose petals on the floor.*
ELIZABETH *enters. She is dressed to meet the public: full make-up, hair and dress. As she enters, they all curtsey deeply.* WALSINGHAM *bows.*

WAITING LADIES. God save Your Majesty.

ELIZABETH. My Lord Walsingham.

WALSINGHAM. God save Your Majesty.

ELIZABETH. Norfolk? What brings you here?

THOMAS. Your Majesty. I am overjoyed to be back in your royal presence. My heart overflows with gladness / to be –

ELIZABETH. Yes, yes – no doubt – but what do you *want*?

THOMAS. To bring you this, madam.

He produces a jar of marmalade, with a flourish.

ELIZABETH. Marmalade.

THOMAS. From Spain, Your Majesty. With almonds and cinnamon.

ELIZABETH. My sister used to eat marmalade every day.

THOMAS. It is indeed the food of royalty, Your Majesty –

ELIZABETH. She thought it would help her have a child.

THOMAS (*horrified*). Oh – that was not why I – I mean – I did not bring you marmalade because I thought –

ELIZABETH. That it would bring about an immaculate conception?

THOMAS *is deeply embarrassed. The* WAITING LADIES *giggle.*

Don't worry, Thomas. I'm the Virgin Queen, not the Virgin Mary.

THOMAS. Yes. Well…

ELIZABETH. My lord, I appreciate your service on my behalf, but please do not trouble yourself to overcommit your stay within my presence longer than might be convenient.

THOMAS *is confused. The* WAITING LADIES *giggle again.*

WAITING LADY. You can go.

THOMAS (*offended*). Your wish is my command.

ELIZABETH (*relenting a little*). Perhaps you would join us at supper?

THOMAS (*with dignity*). I would be honoured, Your Majesty.

THOMAS *exits.*

ELIZABETH. Is it me, or is that the third jar of marmalade in a month?

WAITING LADY. The fourth, Your Majesty.

ELIZABETH. There are no limits to the nobility's faith in the power of citrus.

She dips her finger in the jar and tastes the marmalade. She likes sweet foods.

Mmm. I feel fruitful already.

Walsingham.

WALSINGHAM. Your Majesty.

ELIZABETH. Tell me the news of Mary.

WALSINGHAM. She has arrived safely at Tutbury Castle.

ELIZABETH. In good health?

WALSINGHAM. She complains of a pain in her side. No one knows the cause.

ELIZABETH. Where is that letter?

One of the WAITING LADIES *holds out a letter for* WALSINGHAM *to read.*

Apparently she wants to come to Whitehall. She longs to meet me.

WALSINGHAM (*taking the letter*). Your Majesty, do not consider it.

ELIZABETH. She is my cousin.

WALSINGHAM. You would be contaminated by her misfortune. The people hate her. She married the man that murdered her husband – it makes her appear complicit –

ELIZABETH. Obviously, she should not have married Bothwell, but I cannot believe her guilty of / such a –

WALSINGHAM. Madam, whether or not she is guilty is irrelevant. The point is that the Scots believe she is.

ELIZABETH. But there is an opportunity here. If I could bring Mary and the Scottish nobles together, be the means for restoring her to her throne, she would be dependent upon me.

WALSINGHAM. Your Majesty. Forgive my plain speaking. This is the best thing that has happened to you in a decade. She was your only rival for the throne; and now she is ruined – penniless, mistreated, a hapless prisoner.

Leave her in Tutbury, do not help her, do not permit her to come into your presence, do not restore her, do not allow her to escape.

Pause.

ELIZABETH. Lady Parry, please send for the Bishop of Ross.

WAITING LADY. Yes, Your Majesty.

LADY PARRY *exits.* ELIZABETH *starts to pace angrily.*

WALSINGHAM. I have displeased you.

Beat.

I apologise – I know my words seem harsh, / but –

ELIZABETH. Do you know what they did? They jeered at her as she was carried through the streets. A mob, hurling insults at a monarch. Is that what you endorse? A rabble overthrowing its queen? What sort of precedent does this set? A woman who has finally gained her rightful, God-given throne, through blood and toil and sacrifice, must then be violently treated, because she married someone they don't like?

And you wonder why I don't want to get married.

WALSINGHAM. But, Your Majesty, your situation is / entirely –

ELIZABETH. I will speak to the Bishop of Ross. He is her ambassador, after all. Then I will make up my own mind.

ELIZABETH *exits, followed by the* WAITING LADIES. WALSINGHAM *exits separately.*

Scene Seven

Tutbury. Enter GEORGE.

GEORGE. When Queen Elizabeth first told me of our royal guest I was honoured, of course, and grateful to be asked. But concerned, nevertheless. The cost, the difficulty, and the social complications of a queen who must be treated with respect, but is still a prisoner. She cannot go where she pleases.

But I have discovered in myself a strength of character I did not know I possessed. You might think I would be bewitched by her charms – she is charming, it is true – something seductive in the graceful way she extends an arm… the gentle threading of the veins on the inside of her elbow…

Beat. He clears his throat.

But I am not charmed at all. I am strong, and determined, and for once, I must confess, I feel truly a man. I have found myself!

Enter MARY 1.

MARY 1. My dear Shrewsbury, it is glorious to be outside – I cannot thank you enough for this.

GEORGE. Your health is everything to me, Your Grace.

MARY 1. What a real man you are! Your wife is a lucky woman.

GEORGE. I am so pleased that the two of you are enjoying your time together. It must be very difficult.

MARY 1. I learned my courage in France and carved my strength in the Scottish mountains.

GEORGE. It is remarkable, what you have suffered.

MARY 1. I do not care for my own griefs, but only for those around me who suffer for my sake.

She winces suddenly.

GEORGE. You have pain?

MARY 1. A little, in my side. An old enemy lies there and makes me weak.

She leans on him.

You are so good to me. A ride in the fresh open air is all I need.

They link arms.

GEORGE. You see?

Not. A bit. Charmed.

He thinks for a moment.

Then they exit.

Scene Eight

BESS 2 *speaks to the audience.*

BESS 1 *is waiting impatiently for something.*

BESS 2. Before she came, I never stopped to wonder who I
was. I have barely looked in the mirror since I was a girl. I
always thought: there is nothing that cannot be solved with
expensive clothes and a stern look. I have been the most
powerful person in the room for so long, I fell into the trap of
thinking power belonged to me no matter where I went. But
how can you lead a household when there is a queen in it?

So I looked today. At my face. And then I understood why
George looks at Mary in that way. Nobody would choose
exhaustion over light.

Enter a SERVANT, *at a run.*

BESS 1. What happened?

SERVANT. She ran off!

BESS 1. What? Where?

SERVANT. Her horse just went galloping across the field. The
Earl has gone after her.

BESS 1. He must bring her back!

SERVANT. He is, madam. Look – here he comes.

Enter GEORGE, *out of breath.*

BESS 1. George – where did she go?

GEORGE. She's quite a horsewoman!

BESS 1. Yes, yes, I know that – where is she? Has she escaped?

GEORGE. No – no –

BESS 1. Where is she?

GEORGE. By heaven, don't shriek, Bess! She galloped for a
bit –

BESS 1. Why didn't you stay with her?

GEORGE. She – well – she took me by surprise – and her horse was – I don't know really –

BESS 1. Are you trying to tell me that she rides faster than four men?

GEORGE. Well – I suppose so –

BESS 1. That's it. She is not to ride again.

Enter MARY 1 *and* LIVINGSTON. *They are laughing and exhilarated by their ride.*

MARY 1. We overtook you, my lord!

GEORGE. I must say – you did –

BESS 1. Your Grace. This cannot happen.

MARY 1. Oh, but it was just fun, wasn't it?

BESS 1. No. You could have…

Beat.

MARY 1. I could have what?

Beat.

Did you think I would escape?

Beat.

BESS 1. Your Grace. I am very sorry to report that we have received instructions just now from Lord Walsingham that you are not to ride out again. He fears for the safety of your person.

MARY 1. But I need it. I need the air –

BESS 1. Nevertheless, I regret to say that you must stay indoors for the time being. I will see that alternative occupations are arranged for you to fill the time agreeably.

Please excuse me.

BESS 1 *and the* SERVANT *exit, leaving* GEORGE *and* MARY 1 *alone.*

MARY 1. You were a long way behind. I could have escaped. But I did not.

GEORGE. I know.

MARY 1. It was intoxicating – did you feel it too? The thunder of the hooves and the beating of my heart. And now I have made your dear wife angry.

GEORGE. Oh – no – she's not –

MARY 1. She's not like us, is she? We both have impetuous, perhaps foolish natures, you and I. She is altogether more sensible. I like her very much. In other circumstances, I believe we would all have been friends, don't you think?

GEORGE. Yes – of course, Your Grace –

MARY 1. But I am not myself. I apologise.

I apologise to you both.

She bows her head.

He cannot bear her unhappiness.

GEORGE. I wish there was something I could do to make your life more pleasant here.

MARY 1. You already do so much.

GEORGE. At the very least, madam, let me assure you of my implicit trust in your good faith. There shall be no watching you under my roof – you are our guest. My guest.

MARY 1. Thank you, my lord.

They exit together.

End of Act One.

ACT TWO

Scene One

BESS 1, MARY 1, SEATON, LIVINGSTON, *and* CECILY *are all seated, sewing.*

ROSE 1 *stands nearby, ready for instructions.*

ROSE 2 *speaks to the audience.*

ROSE 2. So it's decided that the Queen is gonna have to stay indoors, and everyone pretends it'll be fine. Personally, if someone kept me a prisoner against my will in a ruddy great castle, stuck in a room with sewers running past the windows, but didn't actually *lock the doors*, after ten days of castrating boredom, I reckon I'd start to consider me options.

For example, opening the door, walking out, stabbing a few guards in the face and making a run for it.

Amazingly, she just sits down, and *sews.*

Silence amongst the women for a while. They sew.

MARY 1. The weather continues mild for the time of year.

BESS 1. Indeed, though Tutbury is plagued by mud from the rain.

Pause.

MARY 1. Did you have much snow this winter?

BESS 1. Thankfully not.

ROSE 2. And this sort of scintillating conversation continues *all day long.*

Enter ELIZABETH, WALSINGHAM *and* JOHN LESLEY. *They move through the room, unseen by* MARY, BESS *and the other women.*

ELIZABETH. So now she has to be kept indoors?

WALSINGHAM. It is for the best, madam.

ELIZABETH. What does she do all day?

LESLEY. She speaks of her love for you –

ELIZABETH. No, no, what does she actually *do*?

LESLEY. Um. She sews, madam.

ELIZABETH. *Sews?*

LESLEY. The practice of embroidery, wherein you take a
needle / and –

ELIZABETH. Don't be an idiot, sir – *why*? Why does she sew?

LESLEY. She is a passionate embroiderer, Your Grace. She
takes great delight in commissioning designs from artists –

ELIZABETH. Designs for what?

LESLEY. Flora and fauna, mostly. For example she stitched a
dolphin, using a picture from a book that she had brought
with her called *Icones Animalium* –

ELIZABETH. Describe it to me, this dolphin.

LESLEY. I have the picture.

LESLEY *gives the picture to* ELIZABETH.

MARY 1. My dear Bess, look at this. (*Shows* BESS 1 *her
embroidery*.) Do you like it?

BESS 1. It is charming.

What do you think, Rose?

She hands the embroidery to ROSE 1.

ROSE 2. A giant fish, brighter than the sky, with its fin sleek
and gleaming, flying through warm seas –

ROSE 1. It's like it's there, in front of you.

BESS 1 (*pleasantly*). Rose is an artist.

Beat. ROSE 1 *is astonished.*

Show the Queen your hands.

ROSE 1*, still baffled, goes to* MARY 1*, who takes her hands.*

MARY 1. Yes, yes indeed, beautiful, graceful hands.

BESS 1. Light fingers.

CECILY *stifles a giggle.* ROSE 1 *wonders if she is about to be stitched up.*

She is new to us, and shy, but you will find her useful, I think.

MARY 1. What can you draw, Rose?

Beat.

BESS 1 (*gently*). Speak.

ROSE 1. I don't think I –

BESS 1. Draw Zenobia.

I think you have it in you.

She hands ROSE 1 *a parchment and quill.*

ROSE 1, *with much hesitation, starts to draw.*

ROSE 2. I never held a quill in my life. But I've just learnt that I have graceful hands! And suddenly it seems the most important thing in the world that I draw that woman with the spear.

ELIZABETH. Dolphins are strange creatures. Are they not, Walsingham?

WALSINGHAM. I found them to be the most charming beasts of the sea, when I saw them off the coast of Portugal.

ELIZABETH. How I would love to see them flying through the air like that! What do you think, my Lord Bishop?

LESLEY. Your Majesty, to a man of God such as I, art is falsehood. It conceals the true nature of a man in a way that surely God did not intend. But, created by a captive queen, in lonely confinement, it has a purity attached that moves the spirit / to pity –

ELIZABETH (*a dismissal*). Thank you.

LESLEY *bows and exits.*

ROSE 1 *is still drawing, rapidly now.*

ROSE 2. My hand is flying across the page, wild and fierce, finding the artist in me. And when I've finished –

ROSE 1 *stares at her handiwork in dismay.*

It's terrible. A scrawling, ridiculous mess.

ROSE 1 *looks around the room. She panics. Screws the parchment up.*

ROSE 1. 'Scuse me.

She rushes out. BESS 1 *is unruffled.*

BESS 1. She's temperamental.

ELIZABETH. Walsingham, I don't like her being cooped up inside. Surely it's enough to send anyone a bit…

I mean, she's just sewing all day…

WALSINGHAM. I think it's excellent, Your Majesty. She is a dangerous woman, but even I cannot think of any threats arising from *embroidery*.

Exit all except MARY 1 *and* LIVINGSTON.

Scene Two

MARY 1 *sits motionless, the embroidery untouched in her lap.* LIVINGSTON *is with her.*

Enter MARY 2. *She speaks to the audience.*

MARY 2. I become used to the cold walls around me. To the feeling of stasis, the certainty that we will be here in this mouldy place for ever.

I write to the Spanish Ambassador several times, asking for aid. I write to my brother, desperate for news of my baby son and my kingdom. I do not receive any replies.

Perhaps the mud has swallowed up the rest of the world.

Perhaps I will die here, having never been anything, after all.

Enter SEATON, *with* LESLEY.

SEATON. Your Grace – the Bishop of Ross has returned from Whitehall.

MARY 1. John!

LESLEY (*bowing*). Your Grace.

MARY 1. What was it like?

LESLEY. It is certainly an impressive palace. There are two thousand rooms.

LIVINGSTON. Two thousand!

LESLEY. Though many of them are small. The decorations are superb – there is a portrait of King Henry VIII on the wall that is larger than the man himself – rather confusing if you happen upon it, because you think you've seen a ghost.

They cross themselves.

MARY 1. Tell me everything she said.

LESLEY. She asked about your habits. I told her about the embroidery. She seemed concerned for your welfare. She worried that you did not have enough to do all day.

MARY 1. Did she change her mind about me staying indoors?

LESLEY. I'm afraid not, Your Grace. Walsingham was there, and I think he is not an advocate of your cause.

MARY 1. He is a hateful man. Afraid of the true faith.

LESLEY. Your Grace, there is something else. I met the Duke of Norfolk in Whitehall, and we spoke.

MARY 1. Norfolk? He has written to me before, he is sympathetic to us.

LESLEY. More than sympathetic – while he was in York earlier in the year he was approached by several nobles who suggested that he… unite with you.

MARY 1. Unite?

LESLEY. In marriage, Your Grace. They say your present marriage can be annulled.

MARY 1. Which nobles?

LESLEY. The Earls of Leicester and of Pembroke are in favour.
    And the Scottish Regent.

MARY 1. My brother agrees?

LESLEY. He says, if the marriage were to take place, he would
    support your restoration to the Scottish throne.

MARY 1. What does the Queen say?

LESLEY. She has not yet been approached. Norfolk feels the
    time is not right – he is courting her good will and when
    appropriate, he will delicately ask her permission.

MARY 1. I do not require the permission of anyone to marry.

LESLEY. But he does, madam. It would be dangerous for you
    to go ahead without her consent.

MARY 1. How timid these men are!

LESLEY. I saw it for myself, Your Grace, the Queen is a
    fearsome woman. She knows her own mind.

MARY 1. What is he like, this duke?

LESLEY. You would like him, I think. He is well-favoured,
    pleasant, the most eligible man in the kingdom. As the cousin
    of Queen Elizabeth, he would expect to be named king.

MARY 1. I see.

LESLEY. I showed him the picture of you and he commented
    most gallantly on your beauty and how your letters showed
    you to be a remarkable, intelligent woman. I think it is a way
    out for us.

MARY 1. It could be done.

LESLEY. I think so too.

MARY 1. I would like to consider it. I will write to friends in
    Scotland and ask them their opinion.

LESLEY. Of course.

MARY 1. I will send you word of my decision.

    They exit.

Scene Three

BESS 2, BESS 1, *holding a letter, and* GEORGE.

BESS 2. I ask to speak to George in private, after supper.

BESS 1. Cecily has intercepted this letter from Mary.

GEORGE. Intercepted? We should not be / reading –

BESS 1. I think you should look at it.

> *She hands him the letter. She watches him reading it, while* BESS 2 *talks to the audience.*

BESS 2. I met George once, when we were children, at a ball. He does not remember it, although he pretends to. I was nobody then.

The room was hot and full and I was not dressed as well as the other girls. My mother whispered in my ear that that boy over there was the future Earl of Shrewsbury. Probably the richest person in the room, and he was only eleven. He was already betrothed to an earl's daughter. For the entire evening, he had to stay with his future bride.

I watched them, standing rigid for hours, gripping each other's hands, looking straight ahead. They never spoke.

That was when I decided that, if possible, if there was ever any chance to marry for love, I would take it. Because pretending is no way to live.

GEORGE. I don't think there is any harm in it.

BESS 1. Have you fully understood what she is saying?

GEORGE. Yes – she fears for her life, of course she does –

BESS 1. She is trying to arrange a marriage, George.

GEORGE. That's impossible –

BESS 1. Read it again.

GEORGE. Her handwriting is lamentable.

BESS 1. It must have been written in haste. I will get it copied and sent to Walsingham.

GEORGE. I don't think we / should –

BESS 1. He insisted he see all her correspondence.

GEORGE. But –

BESS 1. Someone has suggested to her – the Bishop of Ross, I imagine – that a marriage to the Duke of Norfolk might solve all her problems.

GEORGE. The Duke of Norfolk? It's not a *bad* idea.

BESS 1. In which case, telling Walsingham will do no harm.

GEORGE. It will cause unnecessary concern. Perhaps I shall speak to her, ask her not to mention such things under my roof. She seems most reasonable –

BESS 1. Why are you defending her?

GEORGE. I am not – defending –

BESS 1. You should be more cautious –

GEORGE. Bess! This endless questioning of my decisions. I wish it to stop.

Beat.

BESS 1. Forgive me. I'm tired.

GEORGE. You work late too often. You are like a night owl.

BESS 1. That's what William used to say.

Pause. She regrets saying that; he regrets hearing it.

I'm sorry –

GEORGE. Goodnight.

He exits.

BESS 1 *sits, lost in thought.*

BESS 2. I was lucky; I did marry for love.

The problem is, he died, and I had to marry again.

BESS 1. Cecily?

BESS 2. I remember Elizabeth when she was a girl and I was at her Court. The gossiping, the talk of sleeves and skirts. The

Duke of Norfolk used to beg me to mention his name in her presence. What power we had then, and we did not know it!

Now he plots her overthrow, while others turn a blind eye because they are infatuated. I do not see why she should be kept in the dark.

Enter CECILY.

CECILY. Yes, my lady?

BESS 1. Please deliver this to Lord Walsingham's man in The Dog and Partridge tomorrow morning. Don't tell anyone.

CECILY. Very good, madam.

Exit CECILY.

BESS 2. She did not choose this. I think she has a right to know what is happening.

Exit BESS 1 *and* BESS 2.

Scene Four

ROSE 2 *talks to the audience.*

ROSE 1 *sits on the floor facing an imaginary picture.*

ROSE 2. It's very odd, being inside all night, when you're used to napping in doorways. I'm supposed to lie down on the floor with the other maids on a sort of straw-pallet thing but I'd never noticed before how weird other people look when they're asleep. Put me off.

So instead, I decide to learn about art. There's paintings and tapestries everywhere and I study them, one by one. It's like a space has opened up in my brain, that wasn't there before, and I fill it with paint and stitches.

This one's a picture of William Cavendish, the Countess's previous husband. Handsome fella: red hair, incredibly curly moustache. I'm noticing the shadows under the nose and in the curls of his ruff. He looks sad, like he knows he's gonna die before his time.

She doesn't sleep either. So sometimes she comes in and we pretend it's all totally normal.

Enter BESS 1. ROSE 1 *jumps up and curtseys.*

ROSE 1. D'you need anything, my lady?

BESS 1. No, thank you, Rose, goodnight.

ROSE 1. Night, madam.

Exit BESS 1.

ROSE 2. But gradually we get used to each other, and we stop pretending. In the daytime she's my mistress and I've got to do whatever she wants, but at night, we're just two cold bodies looking at stuff on a wall.

Enter BESS 1. *She stands behind* ROSE 1 *and they face the audience, looking together at a new tapestry.*

ROSE 1. What's her name?

BESS 1. Penelope.

ROSE 1. Why's she standing like that, with her hand out?

BESS 1. It's a story from Ancient Greece. Her husband, Odysseus, went to war and never came back. For twenty years she waited. She could not believe that he had gone, he was her soul. Without him she thought she was nothing.

Enter GEORGE, *unseen.*

But because she was a queen, they would not leave her alone. They told her she must marry again, spend her nights with another man, even though the very thought –

Grief has flooded BESS 1's *face. Beat.*

The very thought made her shudder.

GEORGE. Bess.

BESS 1 (*guiltily*). Goodnight, Rose.

ROSE 1. Night, my lady.

BESS 1 *exits with* GEORGE. *Before she goes, she hands*
ROSE 1 *a package.*

ROSE 2 (*as* ROSE 1 *looks at the package*). Parchment, quills. I
make a start.

ROSE 1 *sketches. Sometimes her sketches do not work – in
which case she crosses it out and starts again. Sometimes
they are successful.*

Just simple stuff: outline drawings of everything I can find –
fruit from the pantry, the stable cat, a sleeping groom.

I've got this feeling I've not had before. I think it might be
joy.

It's like I've found myself. My voice, or something. And it's
all come from *her*. She's amazing. It's like – she's my real
mother.

The nights go by, and I never get tired. I just draw.

One night, she comes back and starts talking to me again.

Enter BESS 1. *She stands behind* ROSE 1 *and looks at the
picture of Penelope.*

ROSE 1. What happened to Penelope?

BESS 1. She was clever. She told her suitors she would weave a
tapestry for her husband, and when it was finished, she
would marry one of them. Every day she sat by her loom,
weaving, but every night, she crept out and unstitched it.

ROSE 1. And did her fella come back?

BESS 1. Just when she was about to give up hope, he came
home, and they were reunited. They spent the night together,
and in the morning he killed the suitors, every single one.

ROSE 1. S'harsh.

BESS 1. They did not understand, you see, that what is stitched
with a needle is not always innocent. Because the rhythm is
slow, and gentle, and the action performed by a woman, they
were deceived. Needles are dangerous.

Beat.

ROSE 1. I *have* to be an artist.

BESS 1. I know. You will.

ROSE 2. So I practised. And sometimes she was there, watching me.

And once, when I turned round suddenly, I saw tears in her eyes.

ROSE 1 *turns around and looks at* BESS 1.

ROSE 1. Are you alright, my lady?

BESS 1 (*turning away*). Of course.

ROSE 2. And I dunno why, but there's grief there, as thick as these walls.

It's like she's cracking up, and only I can see it.

And I – sort of – *love* her.

BESS 1. Rose. I want to show you something.

ROSE 2. She takes me to a corner of the castle, where there's this door that's normally locked. And we go in.

ROSE 1 *stares at the room. She is astonished.*

Floor to ceiling, wall to wall, shelf after shelf filled with identical boxes.

ROSE 1. What is this?

BESS 1. My accounts room. There's a box for every house, and one for every servant, listed alphabetically by name. Every receipt, every invoice, every household budget for fourteen estates, our children, even our poor lost baby, Temperance. A box for them all.

ROSE 1. But… *why*?

BESS 1. My second husband, William Cavendish, liked to keep careful accounts. He taught me how. At first it just seemed like a good way to remember him, to keep it all going. Once I'd started I couldn't stop.

ROSE 1. Is this what you do all night?

Can't imagine the Earl is all that pleased.

Beat.

BESS 1. How is your progress – can you draw a decent fish, or a tiger?

ROSE 1. I think so.

BESS 1. Well done. I will send you upstairs tomorrow.

ROSE 1. What for?

BESS 1. I believe Mary is trying to arrange a… connection… of some kind.

ROSE 1. Connection?

BESS 1. She inspires devotion. You must find out what she says when I am not in the room. Then at night we will meet here, and you can tell me.

ROSE 1. I dunno if I'm cut out for spying… Not cos I don't wanna help you, I do – it's just… .. She's a *queen*. I mean, she speaks *Latin*. She'll see me coming a mile off.

BESS 1. I need you, Rose. I want you to swear that you will watch her without ceasing, without sleeping, if necessary, and if she so much as dreams a dream, you will tell me.

ROSE 1. Steady on –

BESS 1. We are talking about treason. I need to know if Mary, Queen of Scots dreams of treason. And I need you to trust me. You *must* trust me.

Beat.

ROSE 1. Alright.

ROSE 2. So I make a promise to a countess that I will completely fail to keep.

They exit.

Scene Five

Whitehall, late in the night.

ELIZABETH *and* WALSINGHAM *stride in, followed by the* WAITING LADIES, *who watch helplessly while they row.*

WALSINGHAM. Your Majesty, I urge you to reconsider.

ELIZABETH. It's getting late –

WALSINGHAM. England will not be safe until you are married –

ELIZABETH. Being married is no guarantee of safety. Look at my sister.

WALSINGHAM. But while you are not married, half the country assumes that the next monarch will be Mary, a *Catholic* –

ELIZABETH. I am aware of that –

WALSINGHAM. The first rule of kingship: never give the people an option. If you present them with an alternative ruler, they will feel obliged to make a choice, and it will not be you. In Tutbury Castle right now is a young woman –

ELIZABETH (*furious*). Less of the young! –

WALSINGHAM (*brutally*). A *young*, charming, *fertile* woman – your cousin – who has married three times already and given birth to a healthy son. It's as if you are *asking* everyone to doubt you.

ELIZABETH. But I do not want it! The pawing and the touching and the getting in the way of my work.

WALSINGHAM. Your private concerns should not –

ELIZABETH. Prevent me from doing my duty. I know.

Beat.

Anyway, what can she do?

WALSINGHAM. There are nobles who think she should marry again.

ELIZABETH. She is married already –

WALSINGHAM. They believe the marriage to Bothwell was forced and she can have it annulled.

ELIZABETH. Who would she – ?

WALSINGHAM. The rumour is. The Duke of Norfolk.

ELIZABETH. Thomas? He would not *dare*.

WALSINGHAM. She has been writing about it in her letters – Lady Shrewsbury has sent copies –

He hands her a letter. She barely glances at it.

ELIZABETH. He would have told me.

WALSINGHAM. Would he?

ELIZABETH. Of course – I am his queen. He is loyal to me, he would never… It would be like stabbing at me while my back is turned.

WALSINGHAM. You should speak to him. If he marries Mary and becomes the King of Scotland he will be in direct competition to your throne.

ELIZABETH. I have the heart and stomach of a king – why is it not enough?

WALSINGHAM. You have the body of a woman, Your Majesty. It is never enough.

Beat.

It grieves me that I vex you. But I have one task in this life, and that is to secure your safety. It is all I think about, from sunrise to night.

ELIZABETH. Your poor wife.

WALSINGHAM. Yes.

Beat.

ELIZABETH. Send for Norfolk.

WALSINGHAM. Thank you.

ELIZABETH. And no more letters. Tell Shrewsbury, all correspondence is forbidden from now on.

WALSINGHAM *bows and exits.*

Pause. ELIZABETH *sags, exhausted.*

Cautiously, the WAITING LADIES *approach her. Gently, they start to peel off her outer clothes, perhaps to loosen her wig, under which her hair is very short or altogether bald. One of them tenderly wipes her face with a cloth, removing the thick white make-up.*

WAITING LADY. This is the moment we are closest to her, when we take off the outer face, and let her skin breathe.

WAITING LADY. She wears lotion to cover up the pockmarks scattered across her face. She doesn't like anyone to see them –

WAITING LADY. Apart from us.

WAITING LADY. We nursed her through the smallpox.

WAITING LADY. So we caught it too.

WAITING LADY. We are all bound together in our scars.

Beat. They look at her. She looks vulnerable, a little afraid, human.

WAITING LADY. She is thinking of Mary.

WAITING LADY. She cannot believe she has imprisoned her own cousin.

WAITING LADY. She is remembering the time she was a prisoner herself, in the Tower of London.

WAITING LADY. Interrogated for hours at a time.

WAITING LADY. Made to kneel in front of men who screamed at her, and hauled her about by the hair, until she felt as though her dignity was a dry stream.

WAITING LADY. We were there with her, you see, so we know.

WAITING LADY. We remember the games she played, just to survive.

WAITING LADY. The letters she wrote, the promises she made, the way she made her guards confused and anxious.

WAITING LADY. And now, she wonders, what games is Mary playing, right now? What is she doing, just to survive?

They help ELIZABETH *offstage, to bed.*

Scene Six

MARY 1 *is huddled on the floor, alone, though* MARY 2 *is with her.*

MARY 2. I am dreaming.

Voices. Noises. Bad deeds that I have witnessed.

I am the History, and it is too much.

I am having dinner, with my friends – suddenly men burst in, with guns and swords and shouting – my husband is one of them – Darnley – he is huge – he is –

Terrifying.

Oh God – I am pregnant with my son.

Darnley says – 'Mary, step to the side' – 'I will not!' – 'Madam, step to the side' – 'How dare you approach your queen, sir, have you forgot yourself?'

I must be strong – they have to think me unafraid – but the child! The child! And suddenly there's an explosion – Darnley is flung onto the floor – his body broken.

And I am being carried through the streets and the people are there – waving at first, but then waves turn to fists, and shouts and jeers – they wish I was dead. My people! They wish me dead!

MARY 1 *cries out.*

MARY 1. I did not do it! I did not do it!

SEATON *rushes in.*

SEATON. What is it, Your Grace, what happened?

MARY 1. I saw it all again – I saw him –

SEATON. It was just a dream –

MARY 1. Blood everywhere...

SEATON (*soothing*). Shhhhhh.

MARY 1. My son, where is my son – ?

SEATON. He is safe, Your Grace, he is safe in Scotland –

MARY 1. I can't breathe here.

SEATON. I know.

MARY 1. These new rules. I'm not allowed out of doors, no letters, no visits, I shall die.

SEATON. No, no –

MARY. I wish to leave.

SEATON. But we can't –

MARY 1. I must. We have to find a way. We have to escape.

SEATON. Your Grace –

MARY 1. I mean it. We will escape.

SEATON *helps* MARY 1 *offstage*.

MARY 2 *follows*.

End of Act Two.

Interval.

ACT THREE

Scene One

SEATON *and* LIVINGSTON *are sewing.*

SEATON *is quiet, patient, stoical.*

LIVINGSTON *is bored. She yawns, stretches her legs.*

SEATON. Sit still.

LIVINGSTON. It's endlessly boring.

SEATON. We are not here to judge, but to *serve*.

LIVINGSTON (*re: the audience*). Can't we chat to them? Tell them our point of view.

SEATON. We do not have a point of view, we are ladies-in-waiting.

LIVINGSTON (*disguising it under a cough*). Chicken.

SEATON. I beg your pardon?

LIVINGSTON. It's alright, everyone knows you're not very good at public speaking.

SEATON. Just because I don't throw myself at people –

LIVINGSTON. *Throw* myself – ?

SEATON. And be all, 'look at my *lady* skills' –

LIVINGSTON. What? I don't –

SEATON. 'I'm such a good dancer, and such a super horse-rider' –

LIVINGSTON. I never say that! Anyway, you're very good at hair.

SEATON. I don't want to be good at *hair*. I want something else.

LIVINGSTON. Like what?

SEATON. Public speaking.

Beat.

LIVINGSTON. Fine.

SEATON. Fine.

LIVINGSTON. *Fine.*

SEATON. Fine!

They turn to the audience.

LIVINGSTON. We're going to give you our point of view now.

SEATON. Together.

LIVINGSTON. After a difficult night, during which Her Grace suffered a terrible nightmare –

SEATON. She woke a little / calmer –

LIVINGSTON. She was pleased when Lady Shrewsbury sent one of her ladies to join us –

SEATON. She's called Rose, but she is not at all like a flower –

LIVINGSTON. Because she was *reputed* to be a fine artist.

SEATON. 'Just what we need,' her Grace said, 'to start on some new designs for our embroidery.'

LIVINGSTON. I was not convinced she'd be any good – but low and behold –

SEATON. She actually was!

LIVINGSTON. She started with an apple tree, every aspect of it from the roots underground to the branches poking at the sky –

SEATON. Bursting with fruit and life and the wonder of nature –

LIVINGSTON. As if she'd spent all her days in the open air!

SEATON. Lady Shrewsbury seemed relieved. What possible subversion could there be in an apple tree?

LIVINGSTON (*getting carried away*). All ripe and lusty and sap-juicy and ready to fall into sin –

SEATON. Stop it.

LIVINGSTON. Sorry.

SEATON. Of course it was only later that we discovered our clever mistress had stitched a secret message in the border –

TOGETHER. Pulchriori detur!

SEATON. Totally brilliant!

They look at the audience expectantly. The audience looks rather blank.

'Pulchriori detur'? 'Let it be given to the fairer'?

(*To* LIVINGSTON.) I don't think they get it.

LIVINGSTON. She's prettier than Queen Elizabeth, obviously. She should have – (*Mouthing the words 'the crown'.*)

She mimes vigorously putting a crown on her head. SEATON nudges and shushes her with a nervous laugh.

SEATON. It's extremely clever.

LIVINGSTON. And no one even noticed!

SEATON. So then, because she got away with that, we suddenly realised: we can *say* things.

LIVINGSTON. Things we are not allowed to put into words.

SEATON. We can sew them. So we tell the strange artist girl to draw the outlines for us, so that we can stitch them. And she does, without saying a word.

LIVINGSTON. A spider, to show the webs we were stuck in. A phoenix, rising up from death.

SEATON. A crocodile, to show that we were ready to slide out of the water and snap our jaws.

LIVINGSTON. And it was like we were bursting out of chains. The boredom, the humiliation, the desperation of our imprisonment. The long hours of silence and waiting, desperate for news but unable to ask for or receive it.

They stand close together.

SEATON. The endless wish that we had the power of a man to make our case, to be heard, because instead we have –

LIVINGSTON. Only us. Just us for so long.

They are holding hands.

SEATON. And we have our love –

LIVINGSTON. For each other –

SEATON. But it has been very sorely tried.

LIVINGSTON. So now we found relief.

SEATON. We told the world who we were, for the first time.

LIVINGSTON. And we were *beasts*.

Scene Two

MARY 1, SEATON *and* LIVINGSTON *sew.* ROSE 1 *is drawing.* ROSE 2 *talks to the audience.*

ROSE 2. I draw all day long, and at night I tell her what they've said.

ROSE 1 *speaks to* BESS 1, *unseen by the others.*

ROSE 1. The two women –

BESS 1. Mary Seaton and Mary Livingston –

ROSE 1. Yeah. They don't really get on. I mean – they do. But they find each other annoying.

SEATON (*pointing to* LIVINGSTON*'s embroidery*). There's no such thing as a pink daffodil.

LIVINGSTON. How do you know? Have you visited every single country in the world?

ROSE 1. And the Queen just talks about the future and Queen Elizabeth. Says she loves her cousin, all that sort of stuff.

BESS 1. Nothing else?

ROSE 1. I don't think they trust me.

BESS 1. Try again tomorrow.

The next day – BESS 1 *and* ROSE 1 *as before*.

ROSE 2. But the next day, it's much the same.

BESS 1. What did she speak of today?

ROSE 1. Her life before. Her husband, Lord Darnley, how he caused her no end of trouble. Always wanting more money, more power.

BESS 1. Did she confess to being involved in his murder?

ROSE 1. No, she seems genuinely shocked by it. Apart from that, we just talked about the sewing. I'm sorry.

Beat.

Maybe she really isn't up to anything.

BESS 1. Try again tomorrow.

The next day. As before.

ROSE 2. And then the next day, we're all busy bees sewing and drawing very quiet, when this happens:

BESS 1 *is suddenly in the room, with an unaccustomed energy and a quiet fury.*

BESS 1. Excuse me, Your Grace, I must speak with Rose as a matter of urgency.

ROSE 1 *rises and walks towards* BESS 1.

ROSE 2. I go with her, just outside the door.

BESS 1 *and* ROSE 1 *go to a side of the stage, while the others sit in silence.*

BESS 1. I want you to give it back.

ROSE 1. What?

BESS 1. Do not speak to me in that insolent way – my ring.

ROSE 1. What ring, my lady?

BESS 1. The ring on the table in the accounts room.

ROSE 1. I haven't got it.

BESS 1. You are the only one that has ever seen it.

ROSE 1. I didn't even notice a ring –

BESS 1. Don't be ridiculous, it was right there on the table. You thought you'd go back to your usual tricks, I suppose, set yourself up for life?

ROSE 1. I didn't –

BESS 1. A glove is one thing. But a ring.

ROSE 1. I made you a promise / that I –

BESS 1. What good is the promise of a thief?

ROSE 1. God! You lot are all the same.

> BESS 1 *slaps* ROSE 1. *A single, stinging blow. The* LADIES *listening are aghast.*

BESS 1. I want you gone from here by nightfall.

> BESS 1 *exits.*

> *Pause.*

> ROSE 1 *is crying. Angry and confused and deeply hurt.*

ROSE 2. Now, ladies and gents, I've been hit quite a lot of times in my life. Me old ma, of course. The landlord of The Dog and Partridge, when he caught me pilfering a loaf of bread from the kitchen. Me ma's New Man, who once got drunk and forgot who I was.

And generally I lived a hungry, cold, and pointless existence until I got picked up by a lady and taken to a castle where I discovered I could draw. And I'd begun to soften, gone off my guard, I'd begun to think I was safe.

So this was the worst. And even now I relive it, again and again.

> BESS 1 *slaps* ROSE 1.

BESS 1. I want you gone from here by nightfall.

> BESS 1 *slaps* ROSE 1.

I want you gone from here by nightfall.

ROSE 2. It was the worst of them all. It's important you understand that.

MARY 1. I would not treat my dog in such a way.

MARY 1, SEATON *and* LIVINGSTON *come to* ROSE 1 *and fold her in their arms. They sit her down.*

SEATON. Poor thing.

LIVINGSTON. Have some wine.

MARY 1. I will not let her throw you out like a chicken carcass. Why does she behave like this?

ROSE 1. Because she's never known what it's like to be hungry more than a day in her whole life put together.

MARY 1. My child, look at me. Did you steal the ring?

ROSE 1. I swear on my life I never even saw it.

MARY 1. Well then, I will take you in. We need your beautiful pictures, I will say that you cannot leave the castle.

ROSE 1. But what if she insists?

MARY 1. If your queen were to die tomorrow then I am the new one. Nobody dares to cross me, just in case.

ROSE 2. So I joined the prisoners upstairs and became one of them, and now, I painted fury onto the canvas.

Scene Three

Whitehall.

ELIZABETH *is there, with a few* WAITING LADIES.

Enter a WAITING LADY *with* THOMAS. *He bows nervously.*

THOMAS. Your Majesty. You sent for me.

ELIZABETH. Three days ago.

THOMAS. I was not well – forgive me.

ELIZABETH. What sort of 'not well'?

THOMAS. An ache in the head, Your Grace.

ELIZABETH. Lady Parry has a migraine at least once a month, but she still attends the Court.

THOMAS. Unfortunately –

ELIZABETH. Tell me about the Queen of Scots.

THOMAS. What… er…. would you wish me to say, Your Grace?

ELIZABETH. Did she, or did she not, kill her husband? Is she busy plotting to overthrow me, as we speak?

THOMAS *hesitates. She switches suddenly from brusque to charming.*

My lord, your confidential advice will be most welcome to me in these difficult times. You see how I am surrounded by idiots here. A man such as yourself can advise me as to how things really are.

THOMAS (*thrilled*). I mean, I can't believe she really is the *type*.

ELIZABETH. That's what *I* said!

THOMAS. A member of your own dear family –

ELIZABETH. Which is yours, of course.

THOMAS. Well, yes, on my mother's side.

Beat. THOMAS *summons up the courage.*

Your Majesty, this feels like a good time to mention something to you –

ELIZABETH. I cannot allow a marriage between you and the Queen of Scots, you know that?

Beat.

THOMAS. I would never dream of such a thing.

ELIZABETH. It must have crossed your mind? A highly desirable bachelor such as yourself?

THOMAS. Your Majesty, I do not like her. The thought of sharing a pillow with a woman suspected of murdering her husband is not appealing.

ELIZABETH. True.

THOMAS. And in any case, madam, consider this: I am richer than Scotland already! I have no need of more lands. Why, I feel king enough standing on my tennis court in Norfolk.

ELIZABETH. What's she like?

THOMAS. Mary?

ELIZABETH. As attractive as they say she is?

THOMAS (*grandly*). Your Majesty, when one has stood before the face of the sun, a planet pales into shadow.

Beat.

It was a – metaphor… The sun is you – and –

ELIZABETH. Yes, yes, thank you. What do we think of planets, these days?

THOMAS. Um… a little bit… dowdy?

ELIZABETH. Dowdy? Yes… I like it…

THOMAS. Like an orange that has gone a bit wrinkly in the sun, and there's a green sort of fuzz around it, and when you taste it, just to see what it's like, you wish you hadn't.

ELIZABETH. Norfolk, you amuse me today! Whoever tried to taste a rotten orange?

THOMAS. No idea! Certainly not me yesterday at dinner.

She laughs, the WAITING LADIES *laugh, they all laugh. And then she is serious.*

ELIZABETH. I thought you had not met her.

Beat.

THOMAS. Well… No –

ELIZABETH. Then how can you know about her looks? How can you know that you do not like her?

THOMAS. I was – just –

ELIZABETH. Flattering me? Trying to say the words you thought I wanted to hear?

Do you think me a fool, sir?

THOMAS. No – not at all – your / maj–

ELIZABETH. Am I here to be lied to? Or am I your sovereign?

THOMAS. I – I –

ELIZABETH. Do you plot, sir? Do you make treasonous plans in the dead of night –

THOMAS. *No!* Your Majesty, I would never –

ELIZABETH. You laugh and joke as though you think you are my favourite – I tell you, if I had one it would not be you, sir. I had rather listen to the Earl of Oxford farting than your tedious gallantry.

The WAITING LADIES *giggle.* THOMAS *is humiliated and outraged.*

THOMAS. But – Your Majesty –

ELIZABETH. That will be all, my lord!

THOMAS *hastily exits.*

ELIZABETH *and her* WAITING LADIES *exit separately.*

Scene Four

Back in Tutbury. ROSE 1 *draws, while* MARY 1, SEATON *and* LIVINGSTON *sew.*

MARY 2. Of course, I know that the artist girl has been sent to spy on me. Strange, quiet little thing, but my goodness, can she draw.

If slapping her was a deliberate ploy to help her gain my trust, it has backfired spectacularly. She is now completely loyal to me.

I watch her drawing with my women, who, it must be said, are starting to seem slightly deranged.

ROSE 1. What about a monkfish – an actual monk, with fins for arms and legs?

LIVINGSTON. Or – a five-legged monster like a rhinoceros lumbering through a jungle.

SEATON. *Or* – a beast with a tail like a squirrel, the body of a tiger, and the face of a goat, stalking the forest with babies curled up on her back.

LIVINGSTON. Brilliant.

MARY 2. And my plan begins to form. I can no longer send a letter. But that does not mean I have to stay silent.

MARY 1. Rose, would you draw something for me?

ROSE 1 *picks up her quill.*

ROSE 1. Yes, Your Grace.

MARY 1. A beautiful orchard in sunlight.

ROSE 1 *starts sketching.*

Apple trees and vine branches. A blue sky and fluffy clouds.

And plunging out of the sky: a giant arm, holding a huge fork, ready to strike at the orchard.

MARY 1 *looks at* ROSE 1's *drawing.*

Add embroidery onto the sleeve of the arm. Like this – (*Shows her own sleeve.*)

And a banner across the front, where I can put a motto.

Lovely.

MARY 1 *starts sewing over* ROSE 1's *outline.*

MARY 2. I sew non-stop from dawn till dusk. I am happy to have a plan at last. It takes a few days, but when it's finished:

MARY 1 *shows her embroidery to the others.*

ROSE 1 *likes it.* SEATON *and* LIVINGSTON *are visibly shocked.*

SEATON (*to the audience*). We know what it is, of course.

LIVINGSTON. And there's a sort of glory to it.

SEATON. But all the same – it's a bit frightening –

LIVINGSTON. Your Grace. Who are you sending that to?

MARY 1. The Duke of Norfolk, of course. He and I are great friends.

LIVINGSTON. But – are you –

SEATON. Accepting his proposal?

LIVINGSTON. Because if so –

SEATON. It's – maybe – a little bit dangerous?

MARY 1. No! It is just a cushion cover, about grief, and loss. The hand represents the way that God strikes at those he loves, even the innocent apple tree in the orchard. I have lost so much, you see, Rose. In any case, I have no means of delivering it.

MARY 2. And then I sit, very sad and still, and let my lies do their work.

MARY 1 *sits very still.*

A story forms in my head. A dream. I have not met the Duke but I picture a handsome, gentle man who will ride up to this terrible place with an army and take me away.

We will return to Scotland with thousands of followers in a blaze of glory. All that I have suffered – all that I have lost – this terrible, aching heart of mine will be healed, as I take back my throne and the people of Scotland welcome me.

ROSE 1. Is she alright?

SEATON. Quite alright.

LIVINGSTON. It's perfectly normal.

MARY 2. And in time, the people of England will realise that their own sterile, empty queen is nothing compared to the vibrant, beautiful Queen of the North. They will invite me – they will beg me – to be their queen too.

As luck would have it, a tear rolls slowly down my face. It's the most tragically brilliant performance I have ever achieved in my life.

Pause.

I am starting to think it hasn't worked.

But then –

ROSE 1. I'll take it for you. I'll deliver it to the Duke of Norfolk, or whatever. I'll do it.

MARY 1. Rose! Would you do that for me?

ROSE 1. Yeah.

SEATON. You brave soul!

LIVINGSTON. What a treasure!

MARY 2. And we hugged her, and I could see her fragile heart breaking with joy to think she finally belonged. And for a moment I felt…

No. If she must be endangered for the sake of the greater good, so be it.

MARY 2 *exits.*

Scene Five

Tutbury, later the same day.

Enter ROSE 2.

SEATON *and* LIVINGSTON *help* ROSE 1 *tie her hair back and dress in male clothing. There is an atmosphere of excitement.*

ROSE 2. Just to be safe, they dress me as a man.

MARY 1. Call yourself Borthwick. It's the name of a castle I have in Scotland.

MARY 1, SEATON *and* LIVINGSTON *exit together.*

ROSE 2. All the other staff have been told not to speak to me, cos I'm a thief. So nobody notices I'm not at dinner, or watches me steal out of the castle. Nobody knows a thing. But even if they did stop me, all I'm carrying is an embroidered cushion cover. It doesn't feel dangerous, just exciting.

I'm good at running through the night, and I'm good at stealing horses. Terrible at riding them. I just cling on to the horse's neck like mad, and follow the moonlight.

Enter LESLEY, *wearing a nightcap.*

I reach Burton upon Trent and the house of Bishop John Lesley, Ambassador to Queen Mary, while he's fast asleep. Safe to say he was not expecting to see a very odd-looking boy in the middle of the night.

ROSE 1 *goes towards* LESLEY.

LESLEY. Good gracious – who on earth are you?

ROSE 1 (*deep voice*). I'm Borthwick. I'm here to give you this.

LESLEY. What is it?

ROSE 1. It's a present for the Duke of Norfolk. Will you take it?

LESLEY. I will see that it reaches him.

He looks at the cushion cover.

God save us – what has she done?

ROSE 1 *stares at him.*

You did well… Borthwick.

ROSE 1. Thanks! (*Remembering she is meant to be a boy.*) Thank you, sir.

ROSE 2. And the Bishop rides straight to the Duke of Norfolk's the very next day, where he is greeted like an old friend.

THOMAS *enters.* LESLEY *turns to him and they shake hands.*

LESLEY. My Lord Duke, this is for you.

THOMAS. There is no letter?

LESLEY. She's not allowed to write letters any more, so she sent this instead.

THOMAS. I don't understand…

LESLEY. Study the picture.

He does.

THOMAS. 'Virescit vulnere virtus.' This means…

LESLEY. She accepts your proposal. You will be king.

THOMAS. Write to Westmoreland and Northumberland. Tell them to prepare the army in the North.

LESLEY. Very good, my lord.

Exit LESLEY.

THOMAS. I will be king.

Exit THOMAS, *with the parcel.*

ROSE 2. But I've already raced back to Tutbury. Returned the horse. Slipped in through the side entrance past the kennels and the sewers. And run quietly upstairs.

It's only then that I remember what the Bishop said:

Enter LESLEY.

LESLEY. God save us. What has she done?

Exit LESLEY.

ROSE 1. Why did he say that?

ROSE 2. Alarm bells start to ring. I suddenly realise: I don't really have a clue what's going on.

ROSE 1. What have you done?

ROSE 2. Or, more to the point:

ROSE 1. What have *I* done?

Scene Six

BESS 1 *is working in the accounts room.*

BESS 2 *watches her.*

BESS 2. For the first time, Rose has not come to the accounts room to report, and I know that something is wrong.

Every so often I see again my hand on the side of her face. It is years since I have hit a servant.

Enter GEORGE.

GEORGE (*mock-formal*). May one enter the hallowed room?

BESS 1. George – I think I have made a mistake.

GEORGE (*jovial*). I doubt it. You are the most efficient accounts-woman I have ever seen.

BESS 1. I have upset one of the maids.

GEORGE. Since when did you ever care for the sensitive feelings of a maid?

BESS 1. You remember the girl I found in Tutbury – the one who turned out able to draw? I asked her to assist the Queen with designs for her embroidery.

GEORGE. Yes?

BESS 1. Each night she has been coming here to tell me what they speak of, so that I am fully / informed –

GEORGE. What? She reports on the Queen's conversations?

BESS 1. Of course.

GEORGE. You are *spying* on her?

BESS 1. Yes, George. At Bolton Castle she made three escape attempts. What did you imagine –

GEORGE. She promised me she would never try to escape.

BESS 1. She doesn't keep her promises! How can you be so / obtuse –

GEORGE. She *promised* – and in return I…

BESS 1. In return, you what?

GEORGE. I swore to respect her privacy.

Beat. BESS 1 *breathes out in frustration.*

You must do the same.

BESS 1. No. She has manipulated you, / George –

GEORGE. That is an order! Good God, Bess, I ask very little of you, but sometimes I wish you would remember your wedding vows. You do a great wrong to treat her with such suspicion. She is a kind, gentle, vulnerable woman.

BESS 1. You like her.

GEORGE. Yes – I like her! –

BESS 1. You *like* her.

Beat.

GEORGE. How dare you?

They are both staring at each other, very angry.

Then GEORGE *exits.*

Pause. BESS 1 *picks up a small piece of material and begins to embroider.*

BESS 2. The Queen of Scots is not the only one capable of sewing fury onto silk.

Pause.

I am sewing a memorial of my own, to a life I have lost.

BESS 1 *hears a quiet noise, and lifts her head. She looks offstage.*

Late, late into the night, I see Cecily slide past the sleeping grooms, and run off into the dark.

Enter CECILY, *holding a candle, with a ring on her finger.*

I worry that she will not be safe. That she will not return at all.

I wonder if I am doing the right thing.

As she goes, I see a glint of candlelight flashing. It's the ring on her finger.

Exit BESS 1 *and* BESS 2.

Scene Seven

CECILY *is alone*.

CECILY. People don't really remember me.

I don't know why.

Even my mother – she had seven children, and I was the last, so maybe she was just tired. She'd look at me vaguely and then say, 'Oh, yes – Cecily.' She left me with Lady Shrewsbury when I was ten and forgot to come back. At first it made me so angry I would punch the earth, but then I realised. It makes me strong.

I listen to everything. Secret conversations in the night. Whispered arguments in the Accounts Room.

I have learned what people want.

The steward, Mr Cromp, pays me a small weekly bonus to know all the servants' gossip. But he doesn't want the truth, just nice things about himself. I told him once I heard Mistress Seaton confess she thought him a fine figure of a man, and he walked about like a cat full of cream for days.

Across England there is a network of spies and informants who report back to Whitehall. Everyone knows this. What people don't expect, is that some of them are women. I didn't know that, until I received my first mission in The Dog and Partridge.

And then all I had to do was to make some friends.

She steps back and watches as SEATON *and* LIVINGSTON *enter. They don't see her at first.*

SEATON (*to the audience*). I have many good qualities. For example: I am a very organised person. I also have an excellent memory and am simply remarkable at quizzes. I possess many other 'quiet' skills that might not be as noticeable as, say –

LIVINGSTON. Being a really good dancer –

SEATON. *Overt*, showy abilities –

LIVINGSTON. Or a super horse-rider –

SEATON. That some men seem to find attractive. Nevertheless, let nobody say I haven't had any offers.

LIVINGSTON. She hasn't had any offers.

SEATON. I have simply turned them down.

LIVINGSTON. I've had six offers.

SEATON. You're married, you're not relevant to this conversation.

LIVINGSTON. Absolutely *inundated*.

SEATON. What I am trying to say… is that I do have… qualities… But I also have a weakness.

LIVINGSTON. Bad dress sense?

SEATON. No –

LIVINGSTON. Your stammer?

SEATON (*baffled*). I don't have a stammer –

LIVINGSTON. A bit boring?

SEATON. Look, this isn't even your bit. I'm trying to tell a story about what happened next with Mary, Queen of Scots and –

LIVINGSTON. Why's it your bit? What bit am I going to get?

SEATON. I don't know – we don't have to do everything together –

LIVINGSTON. Why not? I like it when we do things together…

SEATON. It's getting rather…

LIVINGSTON. What are you trying to say?

SEATON. Nothing. Just. We're together *all* the time…

LIVINGSTON. But it's brought us closer –

SEATON (*infuriated*). You just said I was boring! Can you please *stop interrupting*?

Beat. LIVINGSTON *presses her lips shut.*

After we knew the cushion cover had been safely delivered to the Duke of Norfolk, I was restless, I couldn't sleep. I wandered through the castle, unaccountably full of tears. I was tired, and missed my home, and felt frightened by what we had done.

I met one of the maids, who made me hot spiced milk before asking what was wrong.

And – I told her.

LIVINGSTON *gasps. She backs away from* SEATON *in horror.*

LIVINGSTON. No – you didn't –

SEATON. I'm sorry –

LIVINGSTON. *Why?*

SEATON. I was scared. And she was just… *there*…

LIVINGSTON *rushes offstage.* SEATON *turns to* CECILY *as if seeing her for the first time.*

(*To* CECILY.) It's an orchard, and there's this hand coming down from the sky, and she said it was the hand of God, but it's not, it's *hers*. I recognise the embroidery on the sleeve. It's going to get us all into a lot of trouble.

CECILY. Oh, poor you… So what did it say on the cushion cover?

SEATON. Virescit vulnere virtus.

CECILY. What does that mean, do you think?

SEATON (*looking at* CECILY *with sudden suspicion*). If I thought you spoke Latin I wouldn't have told you. I'm not stupid, you know.

CECILY. I can see that.

She starts to put a cloak on, briskly.

SEATON. What did you say your name was, again?

CECILY *turns her back on* SEATON, *who exits, perturbed.*

CECILY (*to the audience*). It takes me five days to reach Whitehall.

They say that people are overwhelmed when they arrive at the palace, by the size of the tapestries and the shining of the gold. But I have lived with the second-richest woman in England since I was ten years old, I am not scared of wealth. I am not scared of anything.

Nobody even remembers who I am.

Oh, and by the way, I speak excellent Latin.

She remains onstage for the next scene –

Scene Eight

CECILY *kneels. Enter* ELIZABETH *and* WALSINGHAM, *the* WAITING LADIES, *and* COURTIERS.

CECILY. It is a marriage proposal to the Duke of Norfolk, Your Majesty. She has sewn the message into a cushion, with a Latin inscription. The cushion shows an orchard of vines being pruned by a giant female arm, and the inscription reads 'virtue flourishes from its wounds'. The suggestion is that the Duke of Norfolk and Mary will start a new, more fruitful branch of the royal family if Your Majesty no longer lives.

ELIZABETH (*to* WALSINGHAM). You told me there was no harm in embroidery.

WALSINGHAM. I was wrong –

ELIZABETH. Is there a single man in the whole realm who can be relied upon?

WALSINGHAM. Your Majesty, it is worse. The Earls of Northumberland and Westmoreland have banded together to raise a Catholic army in the north. They are heading towards Tutbury Castle now. Their plan is to release Mary and declare war.

Beat. ELIZABETH *breathes*.

WALSINGHAM. Madam, what are your instructions?

ELIZABETH. Close all the ports. Double the guard at Tutbury Castle, and notify Lord Wentworth in East Anglia – tell him to heighten his security and be on alert.

COURTIER. Yes, Your Majesty.

The COURTIER *exits*.

ELIZABETH. Send the Earls of Huntingdon and Hereford to Tutbury to assist Lord and Lady Shrewsbury. While there, search Mary's apartments, collect any evidence and bring it to Whitehall for examination.

COURTIER. Yes, Your Majesty.

The COURTIER *exits*.

WALSINGHAM. What shall I do with Norfolk?

Your Majesty. Do I have your consent to his arrest?

ELIZABETH. Who are they? These men who assume they know better than I? Do they think I look like this by choice? When I dance at a ball, do they think that I dance through merriment? Do they not see I am a puppet, forced to jig to show the world that I am still young? A mask, painted to reassure the world because they must not see my scars.

I tried not to go to war. I tried to tolerate religions different from my own. And because I have wit and a brain and enjoy the sensation of a smile, they think I am a mouse. That because I do not marry six times and murder my kin when it suits me, I have not the strength of my father.

I know how they speak of me. Walsingham – you do it too. Discuss my body as if I am a horse. How and when and if I shall breed. Enough, now. If they do not want a woman as their leader, they shall have a man. If they can stomach a few bones pulled out of their sockets, I can. If they require a battle, I will give it.

But I will always wonder: why could they not let me be the person I wanted to be?

WALSINGHAM. My dear Elizabeth.

They do not care.

Beat.

ELIZABETH. Do it.

WALSINGHAM *exits.*

(*To the audience.*) I have heard the screaming before. I have been the screamer. They have underestimated me, and it will be their end.

Screaming.

LESLEY *is dragged in by* GUARDS. *He is dirty and unkempt. He throws himself at* ELIZABETH'*s feet.*

GUARD. The Bishop of Ross, Your Majesty.

ELIZABETH. Find out everything he knows.

She motions with her head to take him away. The GUARDS *drag him off.*

New GUARDS *enter, dragging* THOMAS.

They throw him on the floor; punching and kicking him. She watches.

THOMAS. Your Majesty –

ELIZABETH. You should not have lied to me, Thomas. I will tell the world what you have done, and the people will hate you. Your lands will be confiscated and your children disinherited. I will ruin you.

THOMAS. Elizabeth – I am – please –

ELIZABETH. Put him in the Tower.

THOMAS *is dragged offstage.*

And if they cannot love me for who I am – if they insist on relentless inspection of my outsides and endless conjecture over the issue of my body – if they cannot find me worthy of affection, I can only give them fear.

Enter MARY 1, SEATON *and* LIVINGSTON. *They do not see* ELIZABETH, *instead they have their hands up and are followed on by* HUNTINGDON *and several* GUARDS. HUNTINGDON *holds a pistol.* LIVINGSTON *and* SEATON *are crying.*

ELIZABETH *backs away a little to watch the scene.*

HUNTINGDON. Search the premises.

The GUARDS *start to search the room.*

Enter BESS 1. *She watches.*

MARY 1. I demand you give your name –

GUARD. Just a load of tapestries, sir.

HUNTINGDON. Collect them up for inspection.

He moves MARY 1 *to the centre of the stage. He starts to feel her body, up and down. She is outraged, but trying to stay calm.*

LIVINGSTON. Get your hands off her!

HUNTINGDON. Be quiet. You're accused of treason, my lady.

MARY 1. I am not a subject. It is impossible for me to commit treason.

HUNTINGDON. You can explain that at your trial.

One of the GUARDS *suddenly holds up a tapestry. It is the one with the apple tree that says 'PULCHRIORI DETUR'. He passes it to* HUNTINGDON.

'Pulchriori Detur'?

HUNTINGDON *approaches her with the pistol. He holds it to her head.*

SEATON *and* LIVINGSTON *are screaming.*

MARY 1. It is an apple tree, my lord! A sad woman's musings, that is all.

BESS 1. Lord Huntingdon. Won't you join us downstairs for some supper? We long to hear the news from court.

Beat. HUNTINGDON *nods and lowers his gun.*

HUNTINGDON. Collect up all the tapestries. They will be used as evidence.

BESS 1 *ushers* HUNTINGDON *and the* GUARDS *offstage.*

A moment of silence after they have gone.

SEATON *and* LIVINGSTON *fall upon* MARY 1. *They huddle together, then kneel on the floor and start to pray.*

On her knees, MARY 1 *looks at* ELIZABETH. *For the first time they make eye contact. For once,* MARY 1 *is genuinely frightened.*

ELIZABETH. You will not die, for now.

But I will keep you in a living hell. Dreaming and plotting of escape and always wondering if there is something else you can try. You can sew until you are half-mad.

I would have loved you, protected you, defended you. But you are the serpent instead of Eve.

MARY 1 *and* ELIZABETH *are finally standing face to face.*

And by God I will expel you from the garden.

Scene Nine

ROSE 1 *and* ROSE 2 *are in the Accounts Room.* ROSE 1 *is hiding.*

ROSE 2. Apparently there's a warrant out for my arrest.

The good thing is, they think I'm a man called Borthwick, so there's a certain amount of confusion.

I'm hiding out in the accounts room, just in case.

Enter BESS 1.

BESS 1. Rose?

ROSE 1 *comes out of her hiding place.*

Thank God.

ROSE 1. They're gonna get me, right? This is it and I'm really going to gaol this time.

BESS 1. No, they're drunk and well fed. They will be fast asleep in a little while.

ROSE 1. I shouldn't have done it –

BESS 1. It's not your fault – (*Hearing a noise.*) hide!

ROSE 1 *quickly hides.*

Enter GEORGE, *rapidly, angrily; he is holding a tapestry, balled up in his hands.*

GEORGE. How is it possible for such a thing to happen? And how did she find out?

BESS 1. George – surely you realise now that Mary cannot be trusted?

GEORGE. The palace is in uproar. The Duke of Norfolk and Bishop of Ross are in the Tower of London.

BESS 1. It will blow over.

GEORGE. I found this.

He holds up the embroidery. BESS 1 *breathes out.*

An embroidery for your dead husband. What did you imagine, that you could hang it up on the walls?

BESS 1. No…

GEORGE. How am I supposed to feel?

BESS 1. I am sorry, George.

GEORGE. I am a good man, you know. I have given you enormous freedom. I think at the very least I might expect a higher degree of respect.

Was it you? That told the Queen about the marriage proposal.

Beat.

BESS 1. Yes.

Beat.

GEORGE. If people knew how it was between us, I would become a laughing stock.

BESS 1. George…

GEORGE. I cannot control my own wife.

BESS 1. It was for the best –

GEORGE. For the *best*? Did you anticipate Her Majesty's heartfelt gratitude? It is the reverse. She says we cannot be trusted. She has cut our allowance. After all that we have done!

BESS 1. I will write to her –

GEORGE. You will do nothing at all.

I leave for Chatsworth in the morning.

GEORGE *hands* BESS 1 *the fabric and exits. She holds it to her face. She closes her eyes.*

BESS 1. You can see it, if you like, Rose…

Awkwardly, ROSE 1 *steps out of the shadows.*

BESS 1 *hands her the embroidery. She looks at it.*

ROSE 2. There's a storm. But instead of rain, it's tears, falling onto quicksand.

All around the border, images of a broken heart: a cracked mirror, a fractured chain, a fraying rope.

And then, in the bottom corner, a glove.

ROSE 1. That's the glove you said I stole. Is that for me?

Beat.

But. You hate me. You *hit* me. You told me to leave.

BESS 1. She would not confide in you, until she saw me cause you pain.

ROSE 1 *is crying.*

ROSE 1. You said I should trust you and I didn't.

BESS 1. Dear Rose.

ROSE 1. I love it.

BESS 1. I'm so sorry.

Fiercely, ROSE 1 *flings her arms around* BESS 1. BESS 1 *is overwhelmed.*

They hold each other for a while.

ROSE 2. She's holding me very tight, I'm a bit crushed, and it's a good feeling. I almost want my arms to break. Then I remember that I'm gonna need them in the future for holding paintbrushes.

ROSE 1 *disentangles herself gently.*

BESS 1. You will have to leave us.

ROSE 1. Yeah, I know.

BESS 1. I will give you what you need to be safe.

ROSE 1. It's alright, I'm used to being on my own.

BESS 1. No, you are an artist now. You will never be alone.

They exit.

Scene Ten

BESS 2, MARY 2, *a* WAITING LADY *and* ROSE 2 *speak directly to the audience.*

BESS 2. For fourteen more years, Mary, Queen of Scots will stay in the care of Bess and her soon-to-be-estranged husband.

WAITING LADY. Eventually she will be tried by her cousin Queen Elizabeth I, found guilty, and executed.

BESS 2. The Duke of Norfolk will be tried for treason. At the trial, the embroidered cushion will be presented as evidence, and he will be found guilty and beheaded.

MARY 2. In two hundred years' time, the embroideries will be found, sewn together into a bedspread, and preserved for centuries to come.

Enter ROSE 1. *She is happy. She feels free.*

ROSE 2. One day, in the pale spring dawn, a thief will slip away from Tutbury Castle without saying goodbye.

BESS 2. She has stolen a pair of boots from one of the footmen, and she's wearing a half-decent dress. In a bag she carries some paintbrushes and canvas. On her finger is a gold ring that means she'll get a free meal at every inn on the road to London, no questions asked.

ROSE 2. On Tutbury High Street, she stops outside The Dog and Partridge and remembers the moment it all began. How will she survive, on her own once again?

BESS 2. The same way that she always did, of course.

ROSE 1 *grins at* BESS 2.

She takes out a beautiful pair of gloves – the same that she was accused of stealing at the beginning.

ROSE 1 *puts the gloves on.*

She starts walking.

The End.

The Glove Thief was first performed by students of Rose Bruford College of Theatre & Performance at Ugly Duck, London, on 15 June 2017, with the following cast:

ROSE 1	Katie Spencer-Blake
ROSE 2	Adriana Moore
BESS 1	Daisy Adams
MARY 1	Jesse Bateson
SEATON / VILLAGER	Alice Renshaw
LIVINGSTON/VILLAGER	Ellie-Jane Goddard
ELIZABETH 1I	Siobhan Bevan
CECILY	Rachel Lemon
BESS 2/ ELIZABETH 2	Billie Hamer
MA/KNOLLYS/MARY 2	Grace Liston
GEORGE/GUARD/ VILLAGER	Jorginho Osuagwu
DUKE OF NORFOLK/ VILLAGER/RIZZIO	Robert Rickman
LESLEY/COURTIER/ VILLAGER/ HUNTINGDON/ LANDLORD	Niall Cullen
MR CROMPE/DARNLEY/ MA'S NEW MAN/GUARD	Tayla Kovacevic-Ebong
WALSINGHAM	James Killeen
Director	Ola Ince
Designer	Elle Rose
Lighting Designer	Harvey Fitzpatrick
Sound Designer	Harvey Allen
Musical Directors	Adriana Moore & Ellie-Jane Goddard
Production Manager	Callum Spalding-Wood
Technical Manager	Sam Jackson
Stage Manager	Martin Johnson

Deputy Stage Manager	Paige Lee Summers
Assistant Stage Manager	Ben Tooth
Head of Sound	Oscar Cotran
Sound Operator	George Hartop
Head of Lighting	James Orr
Lighting Operator	Paul Salmon
Production Electrician	Adam Wileman
Scenic Project Manager	Oli Tratt
Scenic Artists	Rebecca Nicholson & Meggie Settle
Costume Supervisor	Grace Seabrook
Costume Makers	Elise Maynard & Ane Hoel Lotherington
Costume Assistants	Grace Taylor Shaw, Alice Wooding, Molly Bennett, Hannah Liggins, M. K. Morrell & Bethan Price